Making the Impossible Possible

It Is All About Who Is with You

(Transform Yourself into the Best Working
Collaborator God Could Ever Wish to Have)

Fr. Peter Grover, OMV

En Route Books and Media, LLC
Saint Louis, MO

⊕ENROUTE
Make the time

En Route Books and Media, LLC

5705 Rhodes Avenue

St. Louis, MO 63109

Contact us at contactus@enroutebooksandmedia.com

Cover Credit: Sebastian Mahfood using William Blake's *The Ancient of Days setting a Compass to the Earth*. This image has been identified as being free of known restrictions under copyright law, including all related and neighboring rights.

Copyright 2024 Peter Grover

ISBN-13: 979-8-88870-287-1
Library of Congress Control Number: 2024926475

Table of Contents

Foreword

Fr. Michael Gaitley

For six years, I lived in the same religious house as the author of this book. He was the director of the shrine attached to our building, and I was a seminarian. While I and the other seminarians didn't get to spend a lot of time with Fr. Peter, we all admired him. To us, he was both "a real man" and "a real priest."

I've especially loved reading Fr. Peter's new book because I know him. I think you'll love it too, because through it you'll get to know a great man and a great priest.

Two things about Fr. Peter make his book an extraordinary blessing.

First, Fr. Peter's remarkable love for Scripture.

During my time in the seminary, I'd heard that Fr. Peter enrolled in a doctorate program in Sacred Scripture and loved to read the Old Testament in the original Hebrew. But he didn't talk like a scholar — nor did he preach like one.

Every Sunday night, hundreds of college students from places such as Harvard and MIT would crowd into St. Clement Eucharistic Shrine and be transfixed by Fr. Peter's homilies. Why? It wasn't just because he had the thickest Boston accent you'd ever heard, but because he brought the Scriptures to life like nobody I, or likely those students, had ever experienced.

One day, when I was a seminarian, I caught Fr. Peter in a rare moment when he was standing still. Seeing an opportunity to better get to know this extraordinary priest, I asked him just the kind of question a young seminarian would ask, "Fr. Peter, who is your favorite theologian?"

"Hans Urs von Balthasar," he replied.

At that point, I figured he was going to recommend some of the famous Swiss Jesuit's books for me to read.

Instead, he told me the following story: "I once met Balthasar in Rome and told him how much I admired his writings. He responded by telling me not to waste my time with his books but rather to focus on Sacred Scripture."

Father Peter followed that advice. He stopped reading the theologians, took up the Word, and apparently never let it go. Indeed, he loves Scripture like nobody else I know and shares it in this book in a unique way, as one who has made Scripture his life.

The second thing that makes Fr. Peter's book a great blessing to his readers is that he keeps it real. Let me put it this way: While I lived at the seminary in Boston, Fr. Peter always had big bags under his eyes because he was usually up all night on sick calls to the many local hospitals. Then, during the day, he was usually rushing around with his tools or carrying construction materials as he worked on endless renovations at the Shrine or in our large religious house. Finally, on his well-deserved day off he was either tying flies or fishing with his dad.

Because Fr. Peter is rich in human experiences and reflects deeply on those experiences — no doubt, thanks to his rigorous formation in Ignatian spirituality — his stories hit home. They masterfully flesh out profound spiritual lessons, making them vivid, real, and accessible to the reader.

I hope you'll enjoy this book as much as I did as you get to know the Word of God from someone who loves it and lives it deeply.

Michael Gaitely is author of *33 Days to Morning Glory: A Do-It-Yourself Retreat In Preparation for Marian Consecration,* and *Consoling the Heart of Jesus: A Do-It-Yourself Retreat-Inspired by the Spiritual Exercises of St. Ignatius.*

Introduction

One of my professors in the New Testament once said that if you love your job, you will never have to work a day in your life. Every Christian is called. It is indeed a privilege to be a co-worker with God. Then we read the fine print and begin to comprehend the high standards, the "Laws," and the divine expectations. We generally feel that only rare and uncommon individuals qualify, like Mother Teresa or John Paul II. We think that in order to serve God, we must attain extraordinary levels of sacrifice and generosity. That would mean that working for God will be difficult, painful, stressful, and long hours—a job for only the most competent. If this is true, then my Bible instructor would never fill out the job application according to his philosophy of labor: "never work a day in your life."

Basing my insights on Scripture (the source for divine instruction), I will promote and encourage a comprehensive spirituality that is based on God using our limitations to show Himself to the world. Partnership with God is simple, easy, manageable, and even exciting. On our part, we give him access to our gifts, talents, and skills. This means everyone and anyone has a role to play in the divine plan and can be a part of His initiative to save the world, not just the spiritually gifted. Everyone is made to enjoy a sense of accomplishment, and working with God will achieve this objective. The reason is straightforward in Scripture. The following pages will show you that working with God will bring your life simplicity, value, and fulfillment. All this and you will never have to work a day in your life. What exactly does it mean to be a partner with God?

Let's start with David, the king of Israel.

The Philistines were a people of nearly giant-like proportions from the North. They decided to seek a warmer climate, so they packed their bags and journeyed south. As they traveled, they pillaged villages and cities. Along the way, they also picked up knowledge. For example, they learned how to get iron out of rock. From that iron they forged sophisticated weaponry and became the most advanced equipped military power in that age. They never lost a battle until they attacked Egypt. After the defeat, the Philistines settled along the east coast of the Mediterranean and became menacing neighbors to the Israelites.

Goliath's sophisticated protective armor was layered to facilitate the movements of his joints. David refused Saul's breastplate because it didn't fit him. So, David, a shepherd without military experience, a sword, or armor was to face the greatest and biggest warrior among the giant people who possessed the most advanced technology in warfare. The odds against David could not have been greater. Then again, if the two were evenly matched, God would not have been seen as the factor who tipped the scales. And that is why it is such a great story. God shines, the world acknowledges that God is great, and David fulfills his role in God's plan. This all came about because God and David made a great team. That is partnership with the divine.

What exactly did David do to foster this perfect collaboration? David was a shepherd boy who knew how to use a slingshot. After the sheep ate all morning, they would take a nap, and David would be bored. We could imagine him putting up some cans on a rock for some shooting practice. David must have had a lot of free time because he mastered his skill with the slingshot just as kids today with their video games. Then, David simply placed his ability in the service of God. So it's not just God using David, but rather David and God working together. It is both God and David who cooperate to land one smooth stone right between Goliath's eyes.

This is the definition of partnership: It is a story about you with all your limitations who team up with God by putting your talent, skills, and gifts in his service. At the end of this story, God will shine, the world will be blessed, and you will be fulfilled.

The book of Genesis is a collection of stories about dysfunctional families, bad parenting, sibling rivalry, and children with father wounds. Still, God executes his plans perfectly with imperfect people, not in spite of the flaws, but precisely because of them. God shines through partnership with personnel that have shortcomings. That is how God shines. He can do the impossible with us.

Think of it, if you commit, you will have a great working partner that will not allow you to fail, a co-worker that insists, "My yoke is easy, and my burden is light." Christ is the greatest yokemate.

When I was in high school, I worked in my father's construction company. My uncle asked my cousin and me to bring the roofing shingles up on top of the roof. I tossed an eighty-pound bundle on my shoulder and started up the ladder. Just as my cousin was about to reach for a bundle, a pretty, young college girl came by and asked him, "Where is Campion Center?" My helpful cousin told her, "Do you see that building? Behind it there is a road and…." "Where?" she asked. My cousin responded, "Oh, it's not far; I will take you there." So six or seven bundles of shingles later my cousin returned to take up his first. My uncle at that moment yelled from the roof, "Someone get the coffee." My cousin said he had his car so he would go. Fifteen bundles of shingles up on the roof later he came back. You would not want to have my cousin as a work partner. That is why farmers invented the yoke, so one ox does not go under the shady tree having a coffee break while the other poor ox plows the field by himself under the hot sun. The yoke assures that the two oxen work side by side as a unified team, sharing the burden. Jesus tells us, "Come to me; my yoke is easy," which means he is our yoke-mate. I think we forget that we do not carry heavy burdens when we co-partner with Christ.

Not long ago a businessman needed my advice. He told me that his father went to the hospital with chest pains. The doctors assured the son that his dad was stable and would get better. So the son decided to hold off his trip to Florida and delayed his visit for a few days. However, that night, his father took a bad turn and died. Naturally, the son was devastated and carried around with him guilt and regret. He was beating himself up. I had to remind the son that he has a workmate. The son was not in Florida at the time of his dad's death, but his partner was there: the Lord. I can only speculate what the Lord said to the dad before bringing him home to his reward: "Your son was not able to be here, but I am here in his place to help you by taking you to my Father's house. You will be very happy there" We forget that we have a yokemate.

I was with my Dad one afternoon watching golf on TV. Phil Mickelson is about to make a putt. If the ball goes in the hole, he will win the tournament. If it does not, then he will tie and have to play a very talented player in extra rounds. So he walks behind the ball and looks, he steps in front of the ball and looks. There is a lot at stake, so he needs time to absorb information from the undulating landscape between the cup and his ball. After assessing the situation, he puts his putter behind the ball and hits it. We watched the ball as it rolled into the cup. I turned to my father and asked him, "Dad, I know why Mickelson is excited, but why is his caddie so happy?" "Because," he said, "when that ball went into the hole, and he won, the caddie just had his pay doubled." That is what happens when you work for someone who is talented and skilled. Your boss makes a big difference. If you work for a great coach, as we know in New England, you are going to the Super Bowl. If you work for a CEO who is demanding and committed to excellence, you are going to receive benefits, bonuses, and stock options that appreciate in the market. What if God were our boss?

Remember the parable of the master who gives talents to three servants, and one of the servants buries the money? Why does he do that? Because there are a thousand ways to lose money in the ancient world. You can take that five talents in the Gospel and buy a boatload of grain, knowing that your investment will double on its arrival at the next port. If the boat sinks, however, you lose your money. You could take your five talents to the bank, but there is always the risk in the ancient world that the bank will be robbed. You will lose your investment. You can give your money to an investor, and he could be run over by a Roman chariot and again, you lose your talents. The smartest way to secure your money in the ancient world was to dig a hole and bury your money. Everyone did it. Thieves couldn't steal it, the government couldn't tax it, and it couldn't be lost at sea.

So let's say the master comes back and says to the first servant, "Where is my money?" and the servant responds, "I am very sorry, but it is gone. I deposited it in a bank so I could get interest, but they robbed it. The Master says, "You fool, why did you do that? Didn't you know everyone robs banks around here?" Then the master says to the second servant, "Where is my money?" He says, "I invested it by buying wheat in Egypt, and they put it on a boat, and it sank. Your investment is now at the bottom of the ocean." Then the master said, "You fool, didn't you know that this is hurricane season?" He goes to the third servant who buried the money, and he asks, "Where is my money?" And the servant says, "Here it is, safe and sound." Well, look who the hero of the story is? The one who buried the treasure. That is not what happens in Jesus' parable, however. The one who buries his talent is the bad guy. Why? Because he forgot that he had a really good boss. If you don't trust your talented boss, you are not going to get benefits.

A nurse called me one day and said a medical student had been the victim of a hit and run and the parents just arrived from Italy. When I reached the hospital, the nurse asked me if I spoke Italian. I said, "As a matter of fact, I do." I entered a conference room with a long table. Around it were seated doctors, nurses, social workers, and friends from the deceased's school. I met the parents and translated the conversation. I can't imagine what it must be like to have your son or daughter die in a foreign country and you can't talk to anyone. After a long afternoon, the parents asked me for a favor. After I heard what it was, I said I would be honored to do it. The next day, for the first time in my life, I said Mass in Italian and gave my first homily in their native tongue. Most of the people in the chapel did not know what I was saying, only the parents. Needless to say, my message was personal. After the Mass, the parents came up to me, and this is what they said: "We are absolutely convinced that God is going to take care of our daughter the same way He took care of us by sending you."

It took me six years to learn Italian. For six years, I stood in front of Italians with my mouth open and clueless, wondering what the heck they just said. For six years, I pulled Italian dictionaries out of my pocket to look up words. For six years, Italians would say: "Stop, stop talking, you are butchering our beautiful language." For six years, I wondered why I was putting so much time and effort into learning a language that I probably would never use when I returned to the States. Now I know why I had to learn Italian. God wanted me to learn the language so I could help parents in need. Six years to learn enough Italian to say one Mass and write and deliver one crucial message, and it was worth it. I have a great boss. He picked me to do a very important job, and together we partnered to get the job done.

Let me tell you about the best fishing day in my life. Dad and I went to a trout pond one day in early spring, and there was a hatch. Let me tell you about the importance of a hatch to a fly fisherman. Maybe once every twenty years, a fisherman will go to a river or pond, and there will be a hatch. Thousands of bugs crawl out from rocks and vegetation simultaneously and float to the surface of the lake. If they make it to the top without getting eaten by fish, they fly away. The fish haven't eaten all winter so they will be in a feeding frenzy. So there we were during a hatch when fish are taking everything we give them. It was fishing paradise. I had just released another fish and was looking over my shoulders and I saw that my dad walking to the parking lot. Where is he going? When I got to the truck, he already had his waders off; his fly rod was put away. I said, "Dad, you can't leave now. This is the best day we ever had. You have to stay a little longer." Dad said, "The nursing home brings your mother her food at five-o'clock. I want to make sure I am there to help her eat. Now you get back out there and fish." I remember standing on the shoreline, devastated as I watched the truck drive away. That is when God spoke to me. He said, "Peter, I got a request today in the nursing home. An unsung hero—your mother—requested some company. She is lonely today, and I intend to fulfill that wish. I am sending my co-worker to make her day." Apparently, I needed to be reminded that Dad is a partner.

It works two ways. Yes, Dad gave up a great day of fishing for his partnership. Today, Dad is part of a fly-fishing club. There are many days when he out fishes the other members. He catches dozens of fish on days when no one else will even get a strike. The members, who are highly experience, are convinced that he is the most successful fisherman they ever met. They tell me he would be able to catch a five-pound brown trout out of a rain puddle if he simply made the cast. They wonder where he gets his luck. They would never believe me if I told them that there is this "partnership."

If you are beginning to think that I am embellishing (or telling a fish story), then look up Matthew's Gospel where Jesus tells Peter to catch a fish and use the coin in its mouth to pay the temple tax. Note that Jesus tells him to go fishing. He does not tell Peter to climb a high mountain or to look under a boulder to find the coin (and bring a shovel). That would be a lot of work. No, he tells him to go fishing to get the coin. Why fishing? Because fishing is what Peter left behind in order to follow Him. Jesus says the coin will be found in the first fish he catches, presuming that he will continue to hook others. Peter gave up fishing to follow Christ, yet the Lord finds a legitimate reason for Peter to go on a little angling excursion. The burden of the tax has been lightened by the partnership:

"My yoke is easy." Peter will never have to work a day in his life with a partner like Christ.

Can you say that you have kept the Ten Commandments all your life? Can you say that a bad word never came out of your mouth; you never stretched the truth, never looked at someone and had lust in your heart? Can you look Christ in the eye and say I have kept all the commandments? We can all agree that the rich man in the Gospel who looked Jesus in the eye and said, "I have kept all of these commandments since my youth" is a model Israelite. Yet, Jesus says it is easier for a "camel to pass through the eye of a needle than a rich man to enter the kingdom of God." Camels are big animals. If you bring a camel in your kitchen and it stands upright, its head will crash through your ceiling and it will be looking around in the upstairs bedroom. You can't even get a fruit fly in the eye of a needle let alone a camel. Yet, it is still easier for a camel to walk right through that tiny hole than for this righteous man in the Gospel to enter heaven. We are in big trouble. The problem is this, it is not enough to keep the commandments as hard as they are, in addition to that we have to also partner with God. We have to help God take care of others, as my father on a day of a great hatch.

During the clergy sex abuse scandal in 2001, when a priest felt what it was like to have a social stigma, I was invited to a Catholic college in West Virginia to promote vocations to my religious order. They gave me a table at the perfect location, a place where I could be sure to find every student in the school: the cafeteria. Each student in the school must have walked past my table at least four times getting lunch and snacks, and yet not one stopped by to talk to me. I remember hoping that anyone would walk over just to say hello. Toward the end of a long and slow day, I heard a voice say (in a familiar Boston accent), "Pedah, is that you?" I said, "Amy?" It was my old girlfriend. I said to her, "I hope you are not still mad at me for dumping you for the seminary." She said, "After you left I dated a guy who is now my husband, and I said to God, 'Hands off this one.'" Then she started to tell me about her life. She has a beautiful home overlooking the Blue Ridge Mountains. I met her wonderful children. She married a doctor, and I heard all the great things that have happened to her since I last saw her. Then she switched topics and started to talk about me. "Just look at you," she said, "you're a priest." Remembering my social stigma and the fact that no one even approached me all day, I said, "Ya, I guess." She then said this to me, "Think of the people you are going to be able to help." It took my former girlfriend to turn on the light for me in midst that social climate to see with clarity. Is that not the reason why we follow our Lord? We partner with Christ so we are able recognize God at work in their lives.

Take a quick look at Peter. We first learn about Peter when he tells the Lord, "Depart from me for I am a sinful man." I have no doubt that Peter was telling the truth about his sinful life. Jesus asks

Peter to follow Him despite his sinfulness. He leaves the boat, the nets, the crew, the career to follow Jesus. That was a very good decision. Peter will see the greatest events in human history. Peter is going to be there at the times of the most important moments in history. He will be there when Lazarus walks out of the tomb. He will see Jesus take a few loaves of bread and two fish and feed five thousand. He will be on the boat looking out when he sees Jesus walking on water. He will be there when the man born blind says, "I can see." He will be at the Last Supper. Who wouldn't have loved to have had a ticket to that event? He will be there in the Upper Room when Jesus visits on the day of His Resurrection. Peter will be able to say that Jesus is his personal friend because the first thing Jesus says after He rises from the dead is, "Tell Peter." Peter will be there at Pentecost when the Holy Spirit descends upon them in tongues of fire. After, Peter will open his mouth and thousands will be converted to the faith. He will touch a paralyzed beggar at the gate of the Temple and that man will get up and walk.

Peter and the other disciples are the ones who will turn the world upside down. They will have churches and basilicas named after them. Their names, their renown, and their legacy will continue to grow daily for the next two thousand years, reaching to the remotest ends of the earth. Jesus turns to a rich man and He tells him the same words He told Peter, "Follow Me." The man went away sad. We know why he was sad—look at what he missed. If Peter were here today he would tell us, "Do whatever you have to do, but if the Lord invites you to follow Him, you will never regret doing it." Just think of the people you will be able to inspire.

This book is meant to help you build on this relationship. If you are going to commit, you need to know that you are in for a unique and fulfilling experience. Your decision to commit to God will be the best choice you ever made.

Part 1

God

We begin with God. If we are determined to take a chance on the Almighty, we need to know and believe in divine power. Yes, God can do anything, but it is best to be familiar with the details. Such understanding will purge away any doubts. God is the perfect working companion because (1) He prefers to do great things with limited resources, (2) He chooses us, (3) he knows how to turn curses into blessings, and (4) he offers an easy path to salvation. We will look carefully at all four.

Chapter One

God Does Great Things with Limited Resources

Several years ago I went on a whale watch. There were twelve of us to brave the cold temperatures, the fall winds, and the choppy seas. We all huddled inside the cabin with hot chocolate and reading a pamphlet provided by the boating company entitled "Whale Tails." After about an hour of full-speed-ahead-to-nowhere the captain announced, "There she blows at three o'clock!" We all ran outside to the deck. Lo and behold, a whale was rolling in the waves. The announcer seemed pretty happy about the whole thing. (We were guaranteed to see a whale or our money back.) He said, "Oh this is Hurricane. We call her Hurricane because she has a swirl marking on her stomach that looks like storm clouds. Now, we have noticed that Hurricane is gaining some weight. That is because we believe she is about four months pregnant. We are not going to get too close to her because she is a little shy, and we don't want to frighten her." Then he drifted into a lecture about protecting the whales. I said to myself, "Wait a minute. This is one whale in the middle of the ocean. Does this creature have any idea that there is a ship captain who knows her name, her personality, is cognizant of her body weight, and happens to be on a campaign to save her life? If all that is the case, then it is very likely that God knows my name, personality, and is on a campaign to bring about my salvation and resurrection.

Among the ancients it was believed that God was only interested in very big and important matters. Some said that God had the universe to worry about. God had to fix the stars and balance the cosmos making sure the heavenly bodies do not crash into each other, an important task indeed. That is why they called God, "the God of the universe."

Then some of the ancients said, "Actually the most important concern for God was the building of the nations. He is interested in the superpowers, the balance of trade, law, politics and he is only interested in important people like world leaders." That is why they called Him "the God of the nations." They thought that God could not be interested in our little problems and fears. It was a common belief until Moses met God. I think Moses needed to know what was important to God so the prophet asked him, "What is your name?" God did not say he was the "God of the universe" or the "God of the nations." He said, "I am the God of Abraham." Who was Abraham before God made him great? He was a wandering uneducated nomad from Ur. Ur? Where's Ur? Exactly my point. He was a nobody, but he was important to God.

Then God said to Moses, "I am the God of Jacob." Who is Jacob? Jacob stole his older brother's birthright. Nice guy, right? Yes, he is imperfect but still, he is very important to God, enough that God named himself after a faulty individual. What does this tell us? It shows us where God's priorities lie.

A woman came up to me once and said, "My husband and I have been trying to have a baby for a long time. Can you say a prayer?" So I said a prayer and the next thing I know is that the wife is having a baby. Naturally, she wanted to show me the infant. When I saw the baby boy, I laughed because he had fat cheeks with dimples when he smiled. She was so proud of the little guy and his irresistible beaming face at that moment and said, "I never thought it was possible to love another human being so much." I wonder if this miracle baby has any idea how valuable he is and how loved he is. Like that baby, do you or I have any idea how valuable we are?

Jesus was in the synagogue on the Sabbath. He saw a woman who was crippled for eighteen years. That means eighteen years without holding a baby in her arms, eighteen years of not being able to retain a job, eighteen years without contributing to society, eighteen years without a comfortable night sleep, eighteen years and she comes to the synagogue—and the religious leader tells her to come back tomorrow to be cured. Before we appreciate what Jesus said in reply, let me illustrate the absurdity of the leader's statement to the woman with an example.

Let's say the synagogue leader were to walk into the sanctuary on the Sabbath and slip going up the stairs, landing on his arm and breaking it. "Oh, my arm hurts," he says. Then Jesus starts to walk toward him. Do you think the synagogue leader is going tell Jesus to come back tomorrow when it is not the Sabbath? I don't think so. The synagogue leader is going to say "It's okay everyone. Everything is fine. Jesus can cure me even though it is the Sabbath because there is a loophole in the law that states that God can cure important people on the Sabbath." When Jesus sees this woman who is not regarded as very important, He calls her "a daughter of Abraham." That is more prestigious than the rank of a queen. It is certainly higher than a synagogue leader. You cannot attain higher social ground than a daughter of Abraham. That is the answer to the question whether Jesus can cure on the Sabbath. He can cure important and special people of God.

The most insignificant human person is the most important matter to God. This is very different from what the ancients thought. The experts in human development say self-esteem is healthy. They are correct. If I am convinced that God cares because I am valuable, then I am less likely to succumb to discouragement or despair. God prefers happy co-workers

It is Possible for God to Love Imperfect People

When I was young, I had very thick hair. It was a nightmare to cut. My mother would bring me to the barber and tell me, "They are not going to be happy to see you today." One day during my construction years I had to cut some floor studs and plywood. Then, I had to work with sheet rock. After I finished taping the seams, I went to get a fresh haircut. The woman directed me to the chair, and I sat down. She started to comb out my hair and woodchips, plaster dust, and whatever else was living in there fell out. I was a bit embarrassed, and I said to her "Sorry about my hair, I just got out of work." "No problem," she said, "I will just use my junky scissors." After the cut, we went to the cash register. In those days, a haircut cost five dollars so I took out my wallet and gave her a five-dollar bill. Then I handed her another five dollars for her tip. So every time I went to the barbershop, she would say, "It's so nice to see you Mr. Grover. Come take a seat over here." Well, on one occasion, my regular barber was out and a there was a guy instead. I sat down and he combed out my hair before getting started. I could tell he was not happy. I said to him, "Sorry about the hair, I just got out of work, but you can use your junky scissors." He said, "I don't have junky scissors." He never said a word the entire time. When he was done, I gave him his pay plus my usual tip. Two months later I went back to the barbershop. This time both the woman and the guy were there and available. Not only did they both want to cut my hair, but they were fighting over me. We can be badly marred with imperfections and still be wanted, appreciated, and valued. Every friend I have is flawed, but they are kind, generous, patient, and make sacrifices for others. That is the mark of a partnership. Who would not prefer a generous loser over an accomplished tight wad?

In the Kingdom of God, Even the Flawed Have Potential to Greatness

By the way, what is a mustard tree? It is a big oversized weed. If you have a mustard tree in your yard, you are going to rip it out and replace it with something more beautiful. These mustard trees are big, thick, and ugly. Jesus says that the kingdom of heaven is like a mustard seed. Why does Jesus use a weed as an analogy for the Kingdom of God? You would think that He would come up with something a little more majestic like a great cedar of Lebanon or the glorious California redwood. Why a mustard tree? Because in the Kingdom of God, even a weed has potential to greatness.

So there is an eagle chasing a small sparrow. Just before the little bird becomes someone's lunch it sees the mustard tree and darts inside. The eagle says, "I'm not going into that thick mess." The sparrow is saved. Look at a rabbit. It has nothing to protect itself. It doesn't have wings to fly, it can't climb trees, and it doesn't have sharp, scary teeth, but it does have a mustard tree. Even a weed has the potential for greatness.

Dad planted his vegetable garden next to the old chicken coop. Naturally, the earth was well fertilized, so the vegetables grew like they were on steroids. So did the weeds. Every Saturday I would go and weed the garden. One Saturday while I was on all fours in the garden, the neighbor came to see what I was doing. He drove a semi-truck, a barrel-chested guy with a thick beard. He asked me, "What are you doing?" I said, "I am weeding the garden." "Why are you doing that?" he replied. I said, "So the vegetables will grow better." He said, "You are wasting your time, they grow just fine with the weeds. Take a look at my garden." I said, "What garden?" He pointed to a field of weeds that was about chest high and said, "Over there." We walked over and using his hands to make a path through the waist high field grass he said, "I know there is a tomato plant around here somewhere." Sure enough, he found one hidden in the weeds, and it was covered with tomatoes. I said, "How is that possible?" He said, "Camouflage, even the animals can't find it." I learned something that day. This must be what God's garden looks like: a field of weeds but hidden inside are the fruits of the earth. Even weeds have a purpose. But I can't help thinking that it would be nice if God had a garden without weeds. Why doesn't he pull out the weeds? Why does God not opt to have a weeded garden?

On my way to St. John's Seminary to teach class, I stopped at a red light. The guy behind me started to lean on his horn. Apparently, he didn't see the "No Turn on Red" sign. I looked in the rearview mirror to see what the problem was, and I could see he was shaking his finger at me, and it wasn't his index finger. At a moment like that, I wonder why God could not make a perfect world with perfect people. Why doesn't God just take out the weeds in the garden?

I signed up to cook supper, so I went to the grocery store, bought some things, and when I got home, I discovered that I was missing the hamburg. I know I bought it because I checked the receipt. So, I went back to the store, and sure enough, they forgot to put one of the bags in my cart. There it was sitting in the cart of forgotten items. It was another occasion for me to ask why God could not make the world perfect. Why not take out the weeds? And here is the reason why.

Once I was coming back from the hospital; it was a very late call. As I was returning home, I thought, no one is in the grocery store at this hour. I may as well stop and get some food. When I got home, the watermelon was missing. I thought they forgot to put the watermelon in the bag. What? So I went back and complained, "You forgot the watermelon." Sure enough, there was a watermelon in the cart of forgotten items. The next day, I was in the kitchen cutting up the watermelon, and one of the seminarians came in holding a watermelon and said, "Anybody know why there is a watermelon rolling around in the back of the van?" Oops! The reason why God does not pick out the weeds is that I would have been plucked out a long time ago.

Remember Moses? Before God called the greatest of prophets, he was tending the flock at Midian. The reason why he is in Midian is because he is a runaway slave with a rap sheet for murder. There is no lower rung on the status ladder. Couldn't God find someone with some success at life? Why Moses? Because in the kingdom of God, Moses has the potential for greatness.

Peter tells Jesus, "Depart from me for I am a sinful man." Peter was a business man and a sailor. I am sure he was disclosing the truth. So why would Jesus want a sinner to join him. Couldn't Jesus do a little better going to the temple or a synagogue to find a religious leader? Why Peter? Because in the kingdom of God, Peter has the potential for greatness.

We are all flawed, like the mustard tree, but in the kingdom of God we always have the potential for greatness.

It Is Not What We Do That Determines Our Worth...

I was called to fill in as a teacher for a permanent deaconate class. When I arrived, I started to prepare my PowerPoint presentation. I did not know any of the candidates but one of them knew me from a parish mission I gave a few years before. He specifically recalled that I gave his son a twenty-dollar bill during my talk. It was an idea that I took from my confrère when he gave a talk to youth. Before I actually gave the money to the future deacon's son, I threw the twenty on the ground and stepped on it. I asked his son, "Do you still want it even though it is dirty?" He did. I started to hand him the twenty, but I pulled it back and said, "Oh wait." then I crinkled up into a tiny ball. I said, "It is now dirty *and* wrinkled, do you still want it?" As his hands reached to grasp for it, I pulled it back again and rubbed it under my armpit. I asked again, "Do you still want it? It is dirty, wrinkly, and smelly." He took it. Why? Because, he can still use it to go to the movies. Despite its unpleasantries, it did not lose its value. That is why God can still love dirty, smelly sinners because they never lose their value. The future deacon said, "My son has never forgotten the message, and neither have I."

…It Is What We Possess

Someone once described the pitch of the great Yankee closer Mariano Rivera: Take a golf ball and tee it up. Now grab a driver and swing away. Then just about three inches before impact, the ball rolls off the tee. That is a Rivera pitch. Imagine you are in the batter's box. Rivera delivers his pitch, and it is traveling straight at the heart of the plate. This is your pitch, and you are going to hit it out of the park. Just as you commit with your most powerful swing, the ball starts to drop before it arrives at the plate. You either miss the ball or break your bat trying. It is unhittable. That is why Mariano is still considered one of the greatest closers in the game. Did you ever wish you could pitch like he can? I heard that Mariano is a very nice guy, and he probably would be happy to show you how he holds the ball. He could show you the windup and even give you some exercises to strengthen your arm. But Mr. Rivera will never be able to give you his extra-large hands. Mariano will never be able to give you his hand flexibility. Rivera will never be able to give you the ability to remain calm at the end of the game when everything is on the line, and you have to please demanding Yankees fans. He will say to you, "I cannot give you everything, you will need to throw my pitch."

With Christ it is different: He can give you everything you need to live his life.

My father is a great golfer. After he had won a few local tournaments in his age division, he upgraded and got a new set of golf clubs. He gave me the old clubs. Do you recall when the one and three woods were actually made with wood before titanium? I said to my father, "Dad, these clubs are antiques." Dad responded, "When you win a few tournaments with these clubs, then you can upgrade." I wasn't asking for his clubs; I was asking for his swing. I was seeking ability, not an object. There is one person that can give ability.

When Christ walked through the locked doors on the day of His Resurrection, he doesn't say, "Hey, look guys, I rose from the dead, isn't that great." He bequeathed to them a gift. He gave them an ability. He offered them something that would forever transform them to be able to do things they never were able to do in the past.

Before I discuss this gift, let me ask this question: What was the first thing Jesus did when He rose from the dead, before he visited the disciples in the Upper Room, before he encountered Mary, before he rolled up the head piece that went over his head, before the stone was moved? What was the first thing that Jesus did at His Resurrection? He filled his lungs with air. The Greek word for "breath" is "spirit." So, what did the Lord give the disciples in the upper room? The exhale: the resurrected breath. He breathed His Spirit on them. We could not want or ask for anything greater. The resurrected gift is ability to do things that we thought were excusive to

Christ. We can now live his life. We have the power to live his compassion, his generosity. Only Christ can pass on an ability to do something great.

If you are raising money for your school with a bake sale and the wealthiest man in the world comes and says to you, "How can I help your cause?" What are you going to ask him? You are going to invite him to buy a cake? No, you are going to ask him to pay for the school. You should always ask for something that matches the potential of the giver. Why do we not do this with God?

When you ask the Lord for something, make sure it matches the potential of the Giver of Life. Ask for something big. Ask for something that no one else can give you. Ask for his Spirit.

I can go to our Lord and tell Him, "I cannot live Your life. I cannot forgive like You. I will never be generous as You. I will never preach like You, or help people in need like You." He will say to me, "Yes you can. I can give you everything you need to live My life." "…and He breathed on them and said, 'Receive the Holy Spirit.'"

God Gives Us Everything We Need to Realize Our Full Potential

I walked by my church, St. Clement, and took a look at the flower garden that I planted around the church sign. To my dismay, there was a four-foot sumac stock blocking some of the words. My neighbor, who helps with the gardening, was there and I asked, "Where did the weed come from?" He pointed across the street to a sumac tree and said, "A bird probably was over there on the tree eating its lunch and then came over here and sat on your sign to digest. It did its thing, and sowed a sumac seed in your garden." I gave the plight of the seed some thought. I pictured the bird sitting on the sign. Then the seed falls from the bird landing on a bed of soft peat moss mixed with a generous amount of lobster compost that I got for half price from my friend at the nursery. There the seed lies, basking in the morning sun. Then about noontime, it is showered with rain. "Oh, what is this I taste?" asked the seed. "Miracle Grow." No wonder the sumac popped up so quickly. I have the best soil in the city. That is because I give my flowers everything they need to realize their full potential.

Dad and I were in Home Depot one spring day and we each bought a tomato plant. I planted my seedling in our urban courtyard, which is walled in by tall buildings. I watered it faithfully and checked its progress routinely. At the end of the season, I picked a total of four cherry tomatoes. I was over my father's house on a summer day, and he asked me if I would help him pick the tomatoes. "You need help picking the tomatoes?" I asked. He handed me a paper shopping bag. I said, "Really, you think I am going to need a shopping bag to hold all the tomatoes?" When I followed him to the backyard, I was in shock. There were so many tomatoes that he had two-by-sixes holding up the branches. It was not a tomato plant—it was a tree! How was that possible? We both bought the plants at the same place. In fact, we took them off the same shelf. Here is the difference. Dad placed his plant in a field, beside an old chicken coop. You can imagine the rich soil on that fertilized ground. He also has a secret that speeds up the growth process. I am not authorized to share with you the secret because it wouldn't be a secret... Fine, just this once I will let you in on the secret. He puts cow manure in a rain barrel, and every three days he stirs it up and gives the plant a drink. Dad has a tomato tree because he gave his plant everything it needed to realize its full potential.

Let's suppose Dad came over to my place and said, "Do you need a hand picking your tomatoes?" I will say, "No." "Why not?" he would ask, "Let's take a look." And he would go out in the courtyard and see a plant with only three hours of sunlight. The tall buildings permit only a few hours of sunlight. It also means that I can't have a barrel of cow fertilizer in front of my neighbors' windows. Remember the parable of the fig tree in Luke's Gospel. "Just give me a year to fertilize it and dig around it." That would be as if my father replanted my tomato plant at his place. That way he could give it everything it needed to maximize its growth.

During the final year in the seminary, I enrolled in a Scripture class that required the student to have taken at least one year of Hebrew. I was in my third semester of Hebrew, so I was allowed to take the class. On the first day, I arrived a bit early and I was the first student in the class. As the other students arrived, I introduced myself to them. Each one told me that they were doctoral candidates from Jerusalem. Hebrew was their first language. Gulp! I thought: "I can't compete at their level. I have no business playing in their league. Just as it occurred to me that I do not belong in this class, the professor came in and handed out Hebrew texts for us to read out loud and translate. Naturally, the guys from Jerusalem read flawlessly. I, on the other hand, struggled. In fact, at one point I had to apologize for destroying their beautiful language. After class, I went to the professor and told him that I was over my head and that I would just slow down the progress of the class. It was better if I dropped the course. He asked me why I was taking the class. I told him that I would appreciate the Scriptures far more if I were able to read them in the original language. The professor said, "This is exactly the purpose for this class." He highly encouraged me to stick it out. I did.

The following year, I enrolled at another school for a Scripture degree at Princeton. I took a class on the prophet Isaiah. During the class one of the students was having a hard time translating a verse. The professor asked if anyone could help him. I looked around, and no one volunteered, so I raised my hand and said, "The verb you are translating is intransitive, it doesn't have an object and while you are at it, add the verb 'to be' to your translation because it has a passive voice." After class, the guy I helped came over to me and asked, "Where did you learn your Hebrew?" I said, "If you hung out with a class full of guys from Jerusalem who speak Hebrew as their native language, you would learn it pretty fast as well." I have my professor to thank. He never gave up on me. Instead, my professor put me in a place where I would be able to realize my full potential. This is the lesson of the fig tree. God never gives up on us. He instead gives us everything to realize our full potential.

I was thinking about Jesus after His Resurrection. If I were the Lord, the first thing I would have done after the Resurrection would have been to get a new batch of disciples. Get rid of the old ones because they left me to hang. They denied me and betrayed me. I need better disciples. But that is not what Jesus did. The first thing he did was to go back to them and give them everything they needed to realize their full potential. He gave them the Holy Spirit. They will soon go off and change the world. God does not give up on us.

The Human Spirit

Yes, it is true. God gives us "ability." In addition to this, we have the human spirit. I had the privilege of knowing a Vietnamese gentleman. He told me, "I was a young boy in Saigon, after the Americans left, and when the communists took over. In the middle of the night, my father took me, my family, and my grandfather and put us in a boat. We crossed the channel without the use of lights. It was dangerous because of the heavy currents and the numerous rocks that barely broke the surface of the water. Somehow my father managed to navigate the channel and we were able to escape the communist patrol boats who were on the lookout for people like us who were trying to escape. After two years, we finally found one of our distant relatives in the US who could vouch for us, and we were able to get visas to come to the States. When I arrived I had absolutely nothing. I didn't know one word of English, I didn't have any friends, and I didn't even have a toy to play with. Fifteen years later I became a lawyer and passed the bar exam." I said, "That is amazing." He then told me this, "Don't underestimate the human spirit. It is an incredible gift if you use it."

One of the reasons I love to fly fish is because of the mayfly hatch. Mayflies live at the bottom of the river as nymphs. We are not sure when or why but after about four years, they crawl out from under their rocks, and they all float to the surface at just the same time. While they are emerging, they take off—what I like to call—their wet suit. When they get to the surface of the river they pull out their wings, flap them around to dry them off and fly away to meet the love of their lives. They only live for one day so they have to mate and lay the eggs within a twenty-four hour period. After mating, the female mayfly flies upstream, and lays her eggs. The eggs slowly sink in the current until they land on the bottom of the riverbed. Take a guess where the eggs land? They rest at the bottom of the riverbed at the precise rock where the mother just crawled out the day before. How do they know where to lay the eggs on the water? How do they calculate the speed of the water and the sink rate of an egg? All this may be impressive but there is more. After the mother lays the eggs, she spreads her wings over the water. That way the dying mayfly will be highly visible to fish. She floats downstream with the eggs, acting as decoy. She distracts the fish from eating the eggs with her own body. This is all remarkable. She provides a home for her young and heroically offers her life in sacrifice for sake of her future family. If a human imitated the mayfly, it would be an impressive story. Remember the mayfly is a bug. If God can program a bug to do great things, think of what God could do with a tax collector, with an unknown virgin in Nazareth, or with me or you.

It May Never Make Sense to Us, but God Has His Reasons for Wanting Us

I have one company who supplies all my cleaning equipment. I can call and tell them, "The what-do-you-call-it on my red vacuum cleaner broke." Then they will say, "Okay, you need new belts, I'll send them out to you." You can't do that with Home Depot. You call and they want the model number only to later inform you that the vacuum cleaner you bought six months ago has been discontinued. Besides, they don't carry parts.

So I have my one cleaning company and—I will be honest—they are terrible. Awful I should say. I hate to tell you my problems, but I bought a small floor cleaner to wash the floor between the pews in the church. The squiggle blades wore out so I called my one company to replace them. They sent me a pair of four-foot rubber blades. My machine is only 22 inches wide. I called to tell them that the blades are too long. They said, "Cut them." I told them, "Even after I cut them to size, they still don't fit because they belong to a different machine."

Another time the nozzle on the floor washer did not work correctly. Instead of a nice even spray, the water just drooled out. I called and told them that something was wrong. They came and took the floor washer away to fix it. Three weeks later I called to ask them, "Where is my floor washer?" They said they were waiting for a part. They finally brought the machine back, I lugged it upstairs, got it filled with water, pulled out the long extension cord, started the machine, only to discover that after all that, they replaced the wrong valve!

Now you may say to me, "Why don't you just get another cleaning company for your supplies?" Why not dump them for some better service? The answer: I like the people. The woman who owns the company gave me a courtesy call. Home Depot does not do this. She asked how I was doing and if I needed anything. I told her as a matter of fact I could use vacuum cleaner bags. Then she told me it was her eightieth birthday. I said, "You're still working at eighty?" She said, "It keeps me young. By the way, I took a hundred dollars off the last bill. Just don't tell my boys." Like I said, I have my reasons. I support them because they are a family of good people. For me, their likeability overshadows the imperfections. Jesus saw Peter and the other fisherman working hard all night to raise their families. He thought, "I like these men. These are the guys who will be with me during my ministry, and the ones who will continue after me to change the world." God picks us because he likes us. We call it in theology, "divine favor." Notice too that Peter and Andrew just met Jesus and they leave their business to follow him. Who does that? Who leaves everything for a stranger you just meet? There must have been something genuine about Jesus. Jesus sincerely liked the fishermen. Peter and James followed Him as a friend, not a stranger.

When I became the director of St. Clement Shrine in Boston, my dream was to have a pipe organ. I made a big mistake. I mentioned to my friend, Fr. Pierre Paul, the choir director of St. Peter's Basilica in Rome, that I wanted an organ for the choir loft at the church. He said, "Oh, you need to have a large pipe organ. I know an Italian builder who will make you a great organ." I said, "No, it will cost too much." Several months later Pierre visited me in Boston, and he gave me the blueprint (and the price) of the organ that the Italian builder proposed for St. Clement. On paper, there were pipes everywhere, some of which were coming out of the walls. I said, "No! I am not going to spend the rest of my life in debt for half a million dollars. No." Naturally, he was disappointed.

Mysteriously, that same afternoon I got a phone call. "Is this the director of the Shrine?" I said "Yes." "I found the perfect tracker, a pipe organ that will fit in your choir loft." He claimed that he was on the lookout for years to find the right organ for our church. He told

the previous director that he would contact the church once he suc-
ceeded in his quest. I said, "Who is this, and how do you know I was
looking for a pipe organ?" He said, "Never mind that now; just call
this number." So I phoned, and a priest said they were passing papers with a building company on a closed church in Hull, Massachusetts. He informed me that if I wanted the organ, I had to act
quickly. I dragged Fr. Pierre with me that same night, and we saw a
very nice one hundred-year-old tracker. Pierre played it. It was
bright and peppy but needed a little work. He advised me, "Buy it."
I bought it for five thousand dollars.

So there was the pipe organ in pieces on the floor of my church's
basement. The bellows needed new leather, some of the moving
parts required some attention or replacement, and it needed to be
put back together again. I had to hire a pipe organ builder. The
Archdiocese gave me three referrals. I picked a name on the short
list and made a call. The first guy pulled up in new Mercedes-Benz.
I took him downstairs, and he looked at the parts and said, "This
pipe organ is in very bad shape. It is going to take a lot of time to
restore it, and the cost will be high." He wanted seventy-five dollars
an hour, including travel time driving back and forth. At the time, I
thought that was a lot of money, and if I ever need a career change,
I am going to be a pipe organ builder. "Thank you very much," I
said. The second guy pulled up in a brand new Dodge Ram four-
door pick up with raised tires. I brought him downstairs, and he said
exactly what the first guy told me. "This pipe organ is in very bad
shape. It is going to take a lot of time, and it will cost a lot of money."
I said, "Thank you very much."

The third guy pulled up in a rusty Station Wagon. When was the last time you saw a Station Wagon? Twenty, thirty years ago? He went to the back of the car to get something. I followed him and saw a box of tools. I asked, "Are those antiques?" He said, "If you want me to fix your one-hundred-year-old pipe organ then I will need some of the tools the original builders used to build it." I said, "Oh." We went downstairs, and as I was showing him the parts of the pipe organ lying on the floor, I told him that I was a handyman and that I could do some of the low-end work. For instance, I could sand out the scratch marks on the wooden pipes. He went over to the wooden pipes and examined them carefully. He said, "These are not scratch marks. These are signatures etched into the wood." He said, "These are the names of the men who built your pipe organ. I know these people. My grandfather worked with them."

Take a wild guess who you think I hired. Why the third guy? The first two guys looked at the pipe organ as if it was a piece of junk in need of repair. The guy I hired saw a treasure. That is why God always picked losers. Moses had his status problems and a past. Peter was a sinful man. Matthew was a tax collector. Paul was a self-righteous Pharisee. God does not see flaws: He sees a treasure. That is why we cannot use our flawed past as an excuse, or God would never have been able to accomplish anything with a person with a questionable past. We may all be flawed but to God, we have potential to greatness.

Chapter Two

Happiness: Doing What We Were Made to Do

What is the difference between the shoes that you are wearing now and the shoes that are still in your closet? The shoes on your feet are chosen. It also means that the shoes on your feet are happy because they are doing what they were made to do. They were not meant to sit in a ware house or sit on a shelf. So when God chooses us, it means we are happy because we are doing what we were made to do.

Corinth is a city in the middle of Greece. On the far east side of the city is a sea. On the far west side of the city is another sea. Boats would come into the port at Corinth. Sailors would get out of their boat, grab their gear, drag their boat to the other side of the city and continue their trip. By doing this, they would cut out days of traveling around a dangerous peninsula. Somewhere along that ten mile strip of land was one of the first Christian churches that Paul founded. I find that odd because I would think that one of the first Christian communities would have been founded in Bethlehem where Jesus was born. I would think that maybe Nazareth would be another location for a vibrant Christian community of believers or Capernaum where Jesus lived and cured all the sick. Nope. How about the Sea of Galilee where Jesus would get out of the boat, cure the sick and feed five thousand? You would think that Christian churches would have appeared along the shoreline. Not one. Yet, right at the crossroads of the Roman Empire is a church. Why did

Paul choose Corinth? Exposure. He wanted to show the greatness of Christ to the world. The best way for God to shine is to show what he can do with limited resources, and with a mixed bag of misfits who converge at the epicenter of the Roman world. So when Paul wrote the Corinthians, he begins the letter by writing, "God has enriched you." He means that God achieved something that no one would have expected.

Once I made a retreat. Let me introduce you to the staff of three priests. The first was a recovering alcoholic. The personnel office did not know what to do with him so decision makers put him in the retreat house I was about to visit. The second had worked himself into a burnt-out state. He absolutely didn't want to have anything to do with ministry. His only ambition was to ride around on the tractor in the garden. They didn't know what to do with him, so they stuck him in the retreat house. The third was a retired priest. Let me warn you about him. If you hear the dinner bell ring, you better get out of the way because he will run you over. Yet, after dinner, when it is time to do the dishes, paralysis mysteriously strikes him. He can hardly get out of the chair. In a bent over position, he slowly shuffles past the dirty dishes into the TV room. Three losers, three complete mismatched personalities were all assigned to a place no one else wanted to go. I am happy to announce that my retreat was one of the best I ever experienced. The burnt-out priest will make sure your room is clean, the food is delicious, and the flowers in the garden brighten your day. The recovering alcoholic will give a talk and make you laugh, cry, and feel good all over. He will tell you that you can do anything and overcome any difficulty with Christ. The retired priest will listen to you and offer years of wisdom from his experience. By themselves, the three are losers. But with Christ, just make sure you book a year in advance.

Why did God choose Abraham? Why did God go to Mesopotamia and ask Abraham to travel over one thousand miles, as the crow flies, to the Holy Land when He could have chosen someone already there? Why Abraham? Scripture doesn't say. Why did Jesus go to Sea of Galilee to pick His disciples? Why didn't He just go to the local synagogue and find an upright, honest person there? Why didn't He go to the Temple where He could have found a competent teacher who knew Scripture and had the skills necessary to preach the word of God? Why did Jesus go to a tax collector, who was a part of the corrupt system of the Roman IRS? It doesn't say. The Bible leaves clues.

I always try and leave one-half hour earlier in the winter when I have to use one of the cars. Why? Our driveway has a steep incline, and if there are as few as three snowflakes on the driveway, the tires will spin. One early evening, I decided to clean the cars and shovel the driveway so I wouldn't have to get up early in the morning and do it. I finished the job, said Mass, got something to eat, and just before I went to bed I stuck my head out the window to look at my nice work and check on the weather. The cars and the driveway were covered. The snow on the church roof slid off and landed in the driveway. I got my coat and shovel and went back to work. As I was getting started one of my confrères stuck his head out the door and asked what I was doing. I was holding a shovel at the time, so I thought it was obvious as to what I was doing, but I said, "I am shoveling snow." "Why?" he asked. I said, "Because there is snow on the

driveway." Then he said, "I thought you already shoveled the snow."
I said, "I did, but the snow slid off the roof." "Why are you shoveling
at this hour?" "Because," I retorted, "it is going to freeze tonight, and
this wet snow is going to turn to ice." He said, "Oh," and went back
into the house. He asked me every question except the one I wanted
him to ask me: "Do you need a hand?"

About a year later, I thought I better go out and start shoveling.
I got my coat, shovel, and a bucket of salt. I headed to the door armed
and ready to do battle. I opened the door, and I could see that someone already cleaned off the cars and shoveled the snow. I thought,
"Who did this?" It was John Luong, our new seminarian. He knew I
had to go out that evening, so he went out and did it. I was very ap-
preciative, and no good deed goes unpunished, so the formation
team put him in charge of the cars, and he did it happily for nine
years.

I was at John's diaconate ordination. The Cardinal, who presided over the ritual, was talking about how deacons are men of service. He mentioned the word service several times, and I remember
the time that he shoveled the snow for me. That is when my question
was answered, "Why did God pick Abraham?" He chose Abraham
because He knew that Abraham would tell Him, "Yes." Abraham left
God a perception that he would be a good workmate. Abraham was
a man who said yes to service, helped people, and made sacrifices for
others on a regular basis. Abraham gave God a reason to choose
Abraham.

Ezekiel was in a concentration camp in Babylon, and he told a
parable to his fellow prisoners. Here is the parable: God took a
healthy branch and cut it. Technically, the branch has no chance of

survival apart from the tree. This lucky branch is in God's hand. God plants the branch in the ground, and it grows to be the biggest and most fruitful of all the trees. The key to understanding the parable is location. If God planted the branch near the Charles River in Boston, some jogger would probably step on it. If God plants the branch in a forest, the larger trees will block sunlight and use up the water supply. I have a spot in my courtyard next to the poor tomato plant, but God did not plant it there because the high buildings would block the sun for most of the day. He, rather, planted it on top of a mountain where it will get plenty of rain, no joggers to squish it, and no overhanging plants to rob its sunlight. When Ezekiel's fellow prisoners hear that parable, they will say, "If a branch that is cut off from its life source can grow into the most fruitful tree, imagine what God can do with a few faithful prisoners who are transplanted from Jerusalem to Babylon. He could rebuild a nation." That is exactly what happened. And I believe that is how God sees us. He will never give up on us. If God can take a branch and produce a tree bearing abundant fruit and take prisoners and build a thriving nation, imagine what God can do with us.

There was once a guy who lost a million dollars in a company, back when a million dollars was considered a lot of money. He had to meet with the CEO. The man who lost the money said to his boss, "I guess you are going to fire me." The CEO said, "Fire you? Why would I fire you? I just spent a million dollars educating you."

Know This: If God Calls Us, He is Going to Test Us

Why are we any different from Abraham, the father of faith? God called him, but He tested him.

Every year, when I go on the family vacation, I bake a chocolate cake. After about twenty minutes, I open the oven to inspect the progress. Even though it looks done on the outside, I can never tell if the cake is baked enough on the inside. I am not a baker. So I take a knife, and I poke the cake with a knife. If the blade has chocolate sauce on it, I put it back in the oven. I keep poking the cake every few minutes until the knife comes clean. You can tell that I baked the cake because it usually has twenty stab wounds. I test it so I can know what is inside.

I taught a catechism class for eighth graders on Monday at 4:00 in the afternoon. There could not be a worse time to teach teenagers. The first thing I would do on the first day of class is tell them the rules: "No talking while I am talking." So what is the first thing they do immediately after I tell them not to talk while I am talking? They turn to each other and start talking while I am talking. I know what they are doing. They are poking me. They want to know how far they can push me. They want to see if I am a spineless marshmallow or an iron wall. They want to see if there is any bite to the bark. Oh, how I love when they poke the sleeping bear. They make me happy when they want to find out what is inside me. You can be sure that I fixed their wagon wheels. They will not be testing me again.

God Pokes Us

God tested Abraham by telling him to sacrifice his only son. As Abraham was taking his son up the mountain, the son turned to his father Abraham and asked, "Where is the lamb?" Abraham does not tell Isaac, "Funny you should ask that, my son, I guess we have to talk." He doesn't say. "Well, we will have to figure it out when we get there." He tells his son, "God will provide." Abraham may not have known the plan, but he knew that God would provide. When Abraham ascended the top of the mountain, God provided a ram to substitute Abraham's son. Why is God so hard on us at times? Why does he leave Abraham thinking that his only son is about to die? Why does he keep him in the dark until the last second when he draws his knife? God pokes us. He wants to prove our allegiance to Him.

Jesus went to Tyre and Sidon far outside of Jewish territory. Why is Jesus going beyond Jewish territory? There was a mother who needed His help. Her daughter was possessed by a demon. When Jesus finally meets the mother, He says something to her that is strikingly harsh: "It is not right to take the food of the children and throw it to the dogs." Why would Jesus be so offensive and deprecating? Jesus is poking. He wants to find out the depth of her faith. What does God want to see when he pokes us? He wants to know if we categorically believe that God will provide. Jesus chose to help the woman and traveled a great distance to do so. But He also tested her. The woman believed, and God provided. If God chooses us, expect to be tested.

Whenever God Tests Us—And He Will—Just Remember to Say: "God Provides."

Every year on our vacation, we hike to the top of a mountain and camp overnight. One year, I pulled out my duffel bag and started to stuff my gear in it. My brother worked at Eastern Mountain Sports and possessed the most technically advanced outdoor equipment. When he saw my duffel bag, he winced. "You are not taking that up to the mountain. I have an extra back-pack because I just upgraded." The pack he gave me had a nice belt, so it took the weight off my shoulders. I started to stuff the pack, and my brother said, "What is that?" I said, "This is my sleeping bag." He said, "Where did you get that?" I said, "Buy one get one free. This was the free one." He said, "You are going to freeze in that, here take one of mine." Apparently, my brother does a lot of upgrading. Next was the tent. My brother asked if it was waterproof. I said, "That is a good question." Needless to say, we didn't take my tent. I had a great time because I got to use the best gear. I can honestly say my brother provided.

God will do that to us. Did you ever wonder why God does not let us take our stuff with us after we die? It is because we will not need it. You will not need to take your bank account. You may want to alert God that you worked hard to save all that money. And God will say, "You don't need that chump change, I have lots of riches and treasure." You will say, "God will provide." Then God will say to you, "What is that? You will say that is my house. I just spent my entire life building and refurbishing this home." God will say, "That old shack. Leave it because I have much better houses." You will say, "God will provide." Then God will say to you, "What is that? You will say that is my job. It took me years to get this title." Then God will say, "Time for a promotion. I have a better one for you." You will say, "God will provide." God likes to poke us to see if we will say like Abraham, "God will provide." When God chooses you, make sure you are prepared to say "God will provide."

Chapter Three

God Turns Curses into Blessings

I got what I asked for…the flu. Why would I want the flu? One of the priests in our community got sick, and we told him that we have him covered. We convinced him that we would take care of his Masses, Confessions, appointments, etc. "You just get well," we insisted. After a couple of days of "covering" for him, I thought that he must have it pretty good: sleep in late, hot soup for lunch, take a few naps in the afternoon, wake up and work on a few homilies, emails, and in my case finish a few papers. So I got to thinking: I want the flu. Well, I got what I asked for, but it wasn't what I had in mind. The symptoms of my flu were so uncomfortable that I couldn't sleep at night or take naps during the day. The more I could not sleep, the worse the cold progressed. I went to the doctor, and naturally, that didn't help. Finally, I ended up in the emergency room. And I said something I never thought would ever come out of my mouth when the doctor asked me what I wanted. "I want drugs. Give me codeine." I got it, and I slept beautifully that night. I was so happy to get back to work that I will never ask to be sick again.

God is exceptionally good at taking a curse and turning it into a blessing. When the Israelites were in the desert, they were cursed with poisonous snakes for complaining. Yet, God took the curse and turned it into a blessing by way of healing. Remember Adam and Eve? After they were banished from paradise they were cursed: "From now on you will work by the sweat of your brow." Today, we like work. We like to see the results of our hands at the end of the day. we like the paycheck at the end of the week. Work gives us dignity and pays the water bill. We even have a holiday called "Labor Day." One of my father's friends recently said to me, "Your father is too old to be climbing up ladders, he should retire." I replied, "Well maybe he likes to work; maybe the reason he is 91 years old and has the body of a fifty-year-old is because he is active by working every day.

The Thessalonians were getting into trouble with elite politicians of the city. They were acting like busybodies which means they were meddling in places they should avoid. So Paul wrote them a letter. This is what he told them to do. "Work quietly with your hands." Why did Paul tell them that? The stuffy politicians love blue collar workers; they like people who have to do the heavy lifting for them. When Christians work, the politicians don't have to work. Paul's first letter and first advice to the first Christians should give us something to think about, and we should take him at his word. Work quietly, stay under the radar, and the unbelievers will start to like you. If you spew out venomous condemnation against them, they will not like you. It is pretty simple math. Hard work will keep Christians alive, and give them cover from the authorities. God can turn any curse into a blessing.

I love to fly fish, and someone was very nice and gave me an old bamboo fly rod. It is fifty years old, but it still works perfectly. Will you be able to say that about your phone? How is it possible that a bamboo fly rod is in perfect working order after 50 years of hard use? The reason is that the makers of bamboo fly rods get their bamboo only from one field located in southeast China. The reason they are picky about the location is that this particular bamboo must endure the worst weather in the world. Monsoons blow all the time and the stalks of bamboo bend deep in its fearsome wind. When the tempests stops, the bamboo snaps up straight again, and because of the wind, the bamboo produces the strongest fibers in the world. Now you would think that it would be a curse to live in this area of the world where the storms are so strong and frequent. But they make a lot of money on the bamboo. Sometimes we think the difficulty in life is a curse, but maybe it is a blessing.

Look What God Does with the Ultimate Curse: Death

Christ turned the curse of death into a blessing at His Resurrection. My friend, Fr. Jim Nibler, told me that he went to visit a young man who lost his leg in an accident. He figured he could offer him a pray and perhaps give him some encouragement. He knocked on the door and asked if he could come in. The young man said, "Father, come on in." Jim entered and was a little surprised to find him so upbeat after such a devastating accident. The young man explained his optimism. "A stranger walked into my room earlier today and said, 'I saw what happened to you in the news, so I thought I would come in and cheer you up. I know what you must be going through.' I was pretty angry; who did he think he was? How dare this guy think that he knows what I am going through? Then the stranger said, 'I want to show you something.' He pulled up his pants, and I saw his two artificial legs. He said, "I don't have any legs, and yet I walked in here, and you could not even tell. I just wanted to reassure you that you are going to walk again. You are going to get your life back again." This is the message of our risen Lord who stood in front of His disciples: You will get your life back again. Death is no longer an end; it is a door to eternal life. Christ turned the ultimate cures into a blessing.

During the feast of Cana, we discover that it is the job of the groom to supply the wine. That is curious because Jesus seems to be acting like the groom when he provides an abundance of fine vintage wine at this wedding. In the next chapter, John the Baptist says that he is happy to be the best man of the groom. In the very next chapter, amazingly, Jesus, the groom, meets a woman with marital "issues" at one of the ancient wells, a place where a patriarch commonly met his future wife. The woman with marriage concerns meets the bridegroom and engages in a theological discussion about fidelity. When you read the Gospel of John, you probably have asked why there are so many references to marriage. If you can't figure it out the answer, then ask yourself what happens when people get married. People usually have kids after they get married. This is the reason Jesus came, to create children of God and for this reason, he comes to a wedding acting as a groom. The reason I bring up the marriage theme is later in the Gospel, the topic of marriage resurfaces.

Jesus talks to his disciples as if he is a man who wants to get married. On the night before Jesus died, He told His disciples, "I am going to prepare a place for you, and I will come back to you again and take you to myself so that where I am, you also may be." These are precisely the words a young man in the first century would use to propose marriage. He would say this phrase to the girl he wants to marry: "I am going to my father and prepare a place for you and I will come back and take you to myself so that where I am, you also may be." After the proposal, the young man would go back to his father and tell him, "Guess what? I am getting married." Dad would then say, "Oh brother, I better add an extra room to the house for you both." It could take a few days or even weeks to get the room ready. The date for the wedding depends on the father. When dad says the room is ready, it's time. The invitation of the father sets the wedding day in motion. The son gets his pals, and they march into the village of the bride. They will all be playing drums, cymbals, and trumpets as they go because it is a festive day. Everyone in the village would hear the music as they entered. All the engaged young ladies would hear the music and wonder if it is their guy who is coming to get them. The groom finds his bride and brings her to his father's house, and the celebration begins. The party could last for days. That is the picture Jesus wants us to have when He comes to us and brings us to the Father's house. It is a festive day. When my mother died, I pictured her as a bride entering the house of the father. Jesus takes death and turns it into a wedding celebration.

The Book of Ecclesiastes and Death

I enjoy reading the book of Qoheleth, otherwise known as Ecclesiastes. A guy successfully climbs up to the mountain of success. He has more money than he will ever spend, he is a king who rules over many nations so he wields great power, and he has vast wisdom and knowledge. Not many people can claim to have acquired so much in a lifetime. Most of us try to crawl our way up the mountain of success but do not get very far. It would be nice to know what it is like to be at the top. So this successful man writes to us to describe what happens when someone arrives at the top of the world. And this is what he has to say: "Vanity of vanities, all things are vanity." The better translation of the Hebrew is "vapor," not "vanity." The familiar passage should read, "Vapor of vapors, all things are vapor." Vapor has the unique ability to disappear completely before your very eyes. So my question is this, why would the guy on the top of the mountain of success call all his money, his power, and his wisdom vapor? What could cause all of these things to disappear before his very eyes? Death.

In the ancient world, they didn't have YouTube to occupy their time, so they had time to think about things like death. And they wondered what it would be like to die. And this is the answer they come up with: the hearse does not need a trunk for the luggage.

Allow me to give you this analogy. Let's say I am an investor who spent a lifetime making meaningful, calculated risks and wise financial discussions that paid off over a long period. I die a rich man with a lot of money in the bank. After a few years in the afterlife, I decide to check up on my investments. I look down to earth and see, to my dismay, that my relatives blew all of the money on clothes, cars, and parties. I would be pretty upset to see my lifetime achievements used for selfish gratification. If you had to do over, would you not reconsider using your time and skills that would make the world a better place, rather than spoil the relatives. That is the purpose of Ecclesiastes. The book invites us to jump ahead in the future so we can look back at what we are doing today and rethink our goals in life before it is too late. Death is a curse, but death also gives us a reason to live well by prioritizing, making the most of our time. When we die, we want to be fulfilled not empty. Partnership with God provides our life with a path to fulfillment.

The Rich Fool: What Not to DO

In the parable of the rich fool, there is a farmer who has an enormously successful harvest. He builds a bigger barn to hoard his success to himself. He thinks he has future security. But there is no such thing as future security. The certainty of death takes away all future security. That is why God calls him a fool because he thinks he has what he can never possess: future security.

Now let's retell the parable with a happy ending. It will go something like this: There was a farmer who had a rich harvest. He said to himself, "Where am I going to put all of my food; my barns are not big enough, I know what I will do. My neighbor Joe, who has a potato farm, just lost his entire crop to bugs. I will fill up his empty barn, so he has something to live on this year. I just saw Paul at the general store the other day, and I asked him about his wheat field. He told me that his wife got cancer and he had to took care of her. He has no wheat this year. I will fill up his empty barn as well. Then the man said, "God gave me extra this year so I could fill empty barns." He dies, and two years later he looks down and to check out his neighbors. He sees that his neighbors are now filling other people's empty barns. Naturally, the man is happy because he left behind a legacy. He made an impact on the world. Why does God give us gifts, talent, skills, and material wealth? It is not just for us; it is to help fill the emptiness of others. We, like God, are called to turn curses into blessings. After all, we are partners.

I know a retired successful businessman who came to our seminarian scholarship dinner. He wrote out a very generous check. Later I had a chance to talk to him. He told me that he spent his life working hard and was very successful as a result of it. Now that he is retired, he spends his time going to charitable functions, hearing their stories, and making out checks to them. Someone said to him that he is writing too many checks. The rich businessman said, "I have one goal left in life, and that is I want to make sure that when I die, I will be a poor man." I am sure he will have no regrets when he goes to heaven.

Christ Takes the Law That Addresses Curses and Redirects It to Promote Blessings

Growing up, I was the second oldest of five boys. That means I had one brother who was a boss and three brothers who were clueless. It was absolutely impossible to grow up with four brothers and not use the word "idiot." Jesus says in Matthew's Gospel not to call anyone an "idiot." How is it possible to have four brothers and not say that word? Why does Jesus make it so hard?

I grew up minding my own business and all of a sudden I entered puberty, and let me tell you how hard it is not to look at a girl with… No, I don't have to tell you how hard it is because you already know how hard it is. Jesus says whoever even looks at a woman with lust is liable to Gehenna. So this is my question: Why does Jesus make it so hard to fulfill the Law. Why does he add so many "extra details" to the Ten Commandments? Why does he raise the standards and put the Law out of reach for us? He tells us why two chapters later.

Jesus is having dinner with the Pharisees, and he tells them, "Woe to you scribes and Pharisees, you hypocrites, you interpret the Law and place heavy burdens on peoples' shoulders, too heavy to carry." What? Are you kidding me? Look who is talking. Jesus does the same thing. True enough, the Pharisees require us to pay a tax on the cucumber and a head of lettuce. I'll pay the tax because it is a lot easier than what Jesus tells us to do when someone humiliates us in public, which is a slap in the face. In that instance, according to the Lord, we have to turn the other cheek and go through the humiliation again. It is easier to pay a tax on the produce.

Let's be fair. Jesus said he did not come to abolish the Law, nor did he come to offer shortcuts. He came to fulfill the Law, and that means reading the fine print. Jesus goes on to explain that scribes and Pharisees are not hypocrites for placing heavying burdens on peoples' shoulders. Jesus does the same thing. Here is the difference. Pharisees put heavy burdens of the Law on peoples' shoulders "and do not lift a finger to help them." Jesus is different. Jesus makes big demands. True, but he helps lift the burdens. Later, the Lord will say, "come to me all you who are burdened, and I will give you rest, for my yoke is 'easy' and burden light." I want you to remember the word he uses: "easy."

How Easy Can God Make It?

I just got back from some hospital work, and Fr. Jerry said we had a bat in the house. I thought he was kidding, but I turned the corner, and a bat was flying around in the hall downstairs. So I asked myself: "How do you get a bat out of the house?" I went to my con-frères and friends—naturally, they were all experts at getting bats out of houses. They all advised me to shoot it. Knowing that was not a viable option, I called a professional. The exterminator informed me that it was very difficult to get a bat out of a house. He needed to come and do an evaluation, check the gutters for potential openings, and seal off all gaps. I said, "I have a big complex." It sounds like it is going to cost a lot of money. He assured me that the service would come at a high price, but it would be worth it. I then went on YouTube and typed "How to get a bat out of the house." A woman comes on the screen, and she said, "You need to know two things about getting a bat out of your house. First, do not shoot the bat. Second, it is very easy to get a bat out of the house. You could open the window, and the bat will follow the draft of the air out the open-ing. If this does not work, then just let the bat move about until it flies into a room. Isolate the bat by shutting the door. The bat will land on the wall or floor. Approach the bat with a plastic container, and don't worry about the bat flying away. The bat can't see you. Cover the bat with the container and slide a piece of cardboard be-tween the opening of the container and the surface under the bat. Once the bat is in captivity, bring the container outside and let the bat go free. Remember the bat is your friend because he will eat all the nasty mosquitoes around your home." That sounds too easy. Her suggestion oversimplified the problem. Still, I would try. What do I have to lose? Sure enough, the bat flew into the laundry room. I shut the door, and there it was resting on the floor. It was easy. I thought getting the bat out of the house was going to be impossible. Maybe fulfilling the Law is not so hard. Not if we go to the right person.

Remember the Lord's advice. Come to me all you who are burdened (with the details of the Law). "My yoke is easy, and my burden light." Let me say that word again: "Easy." What was the word Jesus used to describe our burdens? "Easy." Life may appear complicated and chaotic, but if you follow the instructions of the right person, life can be easy.

Here is the key to success in life: You have to go to the right person with your burdens. So if you have a few problems, difficulties, and maybe you have a mission impossible, go to the right person. I thought getting the bat out of the house was going to be impossible. I went to the right person, and it was easy. Jesus says come to me because he will give you everything you need to be successful. He gives us an example, incentive, motivation, grace, a Church, the community of believers, faith, and help from above. Jesus offers us everything we need to fulfill the Law easily. In this way Jesus turns the curse of the Law into a blessing. Fulfilling the Law is now possible with Christ as a helper.

Two Law Givers: One Promulgates Laws to Prevent Others from Getting Hurt, The Other Gives Laws So People Will Become Blessed

There is a reason why Christ goes beyond the Ten Commandments, why he allows no shortcuts or watered-down precepts. Jesus insists on fulfilling the Law, because Jesus is the Lawgiver, like Moses was the Lawgiver in the desert.

Moses's life was threatened in infancy by a king; Jesus' life was threatened by a king. Moses left Egypt; Jesus left Egypt with his parents. Moses entered the desert for forty years; Jesus entered the desert for forty days. Moses went up the mountain to deliver the Law; Jesus goes up a mountain to deliver the Law. Moses prepares the people for the Promised Land; Jesus prepares the people for the kingdom of heaven. There are striking similarities between the two. However, there is a difference. Moses gives a Law that will prevent people from suffering. When we steal, people suffer. When we curse, people get hurt. When we kill, family and friends are devastated. When we commit adultery, relations deteriorate. Moses gives a law that will prevent people from becoming cursed with pain.

Jesus, instead, makes additions to provide a new purpose for the Law. Like Moses, he goes up the mountain in Matthew's Gospel and gives us the Law, but it is different from the Ten Commandments. He, instead, offers the Beatitudes. People are blessed when they follow the Beatitudes. When we are peacemakers, people get blessed. When we are meek, people get blessed. When we are poor in spirit, people are blessed. When we hunger or thirst for righteousness, people become blessed.

Transforming Ourselves Means Benefits to Others

Every September, college students move into the city. Boston is inundated with moving vans and U-Hauls. I walked by a truck on my way to help out at a local church one morning, and I saw a sofa on the sidewalk with a young student sitting on it, hunched over with his head buried in his hands. If I could read his mind, I am sure he was thinking: "What did I get myself into? Why would I ever want to do this?" If he wanted my advice, I would have told him, "I know you wish you were back home. You miss your circle of friends, your favorite pizza place, and familiar surroundings. Now you are in a big city, where everything is strange, you do know anyone, and you have no longtime friends to console you. You will be undertaking a huge challenge and if your school is one of the best in the country—this is Boston—your teachers will be making demands. They will hold you to expectations at levels you never knew before. You will be tested. I know this is going to be hard, but you need to do this. The lives of others will be a better place because you decided to leave your comfort zone and mature into a gifted person that will help people. Your children will be blessed because you came here to give it your all. People will be blessed because you became someone with special gifts that will help others."

Christ is not just supporting and defending the Commandments that prevent us from hurting others. In addition to these, he also advances a set of Beatitudes that help and benefit others. They are hard and challenging, but they push us to achieve excellence. We are going to need help and no one better supplies that need than Christ himself. Dependence on Christ is a prerequisite for success. Fulfilling dreams to make the world a better place and making a positive impact will require sacrifice, commitment, and a little help. Divine partnership is essential. In the desert, the Israelites faced difficulties and curses. Their need for God gave them an opportunity to seek, talk, and see God in their lives each day. That is how God turns curses into blessings.

Chapter Four

God Provides a Path to Salvation

Jesus tells a parable of the wicked steward who gets caught stealing from his employer, but who ends up becoming the hero of the story. How does that happen? Bible experts have been debating for centuries, trying to figure out how a bad guy becomes God's model for good behavior. That is the reason the parable is so intriguing to read.

Let me try to explain. The first thing the steward does after he is caught with his hand in the cookie jar is ask a question: "What should I do?" I have heard that same question asked by other wrongdoers in the same Gospel such as the tax collectors when they go to John the Baptist. They ask him "What should we do?" The soldiers, who are known for their cruelty, also ask John, "What should we do?" And then the sinful crowd who seeks to wash their sins away in the waters of baptism asks John, "What should we do?" They all have two things in common. They are imperfect, and they ask John what to do. Apparently, that is the question that all sinners ask. John answers them: "build a road." This is an odd request. Luckily, before John the Baptist is introduced, we have a quote from Isaiah that tells us how to build a road. Before you build the road, you need a level surface. So instead of going around a mountain and then going around a valley, you take the top of the mountain and put it in the valley and then you will have a level surface. No winding turns, no ups and downs, just a direct, straight shot on flat level ground to your destination. In other words, if we take our mountain of wealth or our load of skills, our pile of money or our heap of free time and use them to fill the void of need, then we will be building a road to salvation.

So when the people ask John what they should do, he tells them to take their mountain of material possessions and fill the void of need. If you have extra food, give to those who do not have. If you have an extra t-shirt, give to the person who does not even have a t-shirt. Remember, a t-shirt is the piece of clothing that is closest to the skin. If someone does not have a t-shirt, then that person is naked. That is extreme need. If someone has no food, that is also extreme need. According to Luke, the way you get to heaven is prepare a direct path, fill the voids of need one t-shirt at a time.

Now let's go back to the wicked steward. After he asks "What should I do?" he takes a mountain of wealth and fills the void of extreme need. That means the wicked steward is building his road to salvation. The neediest in the ancient world are those who are in debt. If they cannot pay, their only option is to sell themselves and their families into slavery. This guy helps the needy manage their debt with the excess wealth of his firm, and that is how he becomes a hero. He uses wealth to build a road, by filling the voids of need with surplus wealth.

Chesterton once said, "Children are innocent and therefore love justice, while the rest of us who are wicked, prefer mercy." When I die and go to heaven, and hear the choirs of angels singing and father Abraham with his arms extended to welcome me, I will say "Stop, timeout! Why is everyone so happy to see me? I thought you guys don't like religious leaders." And another guy will die and go to heaven and hear the choirs of angels singing and father Abraham with his arms extended in welcome and say, "Why is everyone so happy to see me? I thought you guys don't like tax collectors." And another person will die and go to heaven and hear the choirs of angels singing and father Abraham with his arms extended in welcome and say, "Why is everyone so happy to see me? I thought you guys don't like divorced people." And another guy will die and go to heaven and hear the choirs of angels singing and father Abraham with his arms extended in welcome and say, "Why is everyone so happy to see me? I thought you guys don't like rich people." And when you die and go to heaven and hear the choirs of angels singing and father Abraham with his arms extended in welcome, and you will say, "Why is everyone so happy to see me? I thought you guys don't like… (fill in the blank here)." We are all flawed, and that is why God provides a road to salvation for all. All we need to do is fill in the void with our surplus wealth. That is partnering with God. We entrust God with simple things like extra food or t-shirts. It does not take much.

Remember the parable of the rich man? There is a deep chasm between the place of torment and Father Abraham. The Father of faith cannot send Lazarus to help the rich man because of the impasse. If the rich man had only used his mountain of wealth to fill the holes of need, he would have filled the chasm and walked over to Abraham himself. Unfortunately, he didn't build the road to salvation. Too bad, because he had plenty of wealth to fill the chasm. The best Abraham can do for the rich man is to advise his brothers to avoid the same fate by listening to the prophets (like Isaiah and

John the Baptist) who give instructions on how to build a road that will eliminate chasms.

My friend invited me to fish with him at the Swift River. The fish are known to be very selective and hard to catch. My friend put on a fly that looked like a white gum-ball. He made a cast and as it drifted down the river a fish gobbled it up. He made three casts and caught three fish. After he landed a third fish, a man walked by, and we asked him how he was doing. He said, "I have been fishing for three days, and I haven't caught a fish yet." So my friend took his white gum-ball off his line and gave it to him, instructing him to cast it upstream and let it drift. He caught a fish on the first cast. At the end of the day, I said to my friend, "That was really nice of you to give him your fly." He said, "I enjoyed watching him catch that fish more than anything else I did today." It did not take much to make someone's day. My friend has hundreds of gumball flies. He bought yarn that cost him a buck and ties them up in seconds on his fly-tying vise.

I am sure the wicked steward must have enjoyed helping those people get out of debt. It would be just as wonderful seeing the face of someone receiving a t-shirt who doesn't have a shirt on his back. Hear Christ tell us, I know you are flawed, but be a hero. Build that road. It doesn't take much, a t-shirt, extra food, relief some debt, or a gumball fly.

God Does Not Like Buried Treasure

Let's discuss the nature of Jesus' parables for a moment. A parable is a simple story about ordinary events: farming, lost sheep, wedding banquets, and so forth. Let's say someone tells a simple story that goes something like this. "Well, I went into the store, and I took out my wallet to see what was there and I saw a one-dollar bill…" Notice that simple stories get boring rather quickly unless you throw in a little zinger. Continuing our boring story, for example, "So I took the dollar out of my wallet and bought a scratch ticket and won a million dollars." Suddenly, by adding an unexpected detail, the story is no longer dull.

Jesus does the same thing. He tells us a simple story and just when you are about to yawn, just as your attention starts to wane, Jesus throws in a "zinger." So let's take a look at the parable of the man who bought land with buried treasure on it. Let's say I am the guy who is going to buy the land so I go to the owner and say, "I would like to buy that small piece of land." He says, "Fine if you want it, that will be $100." Then I reply, "I think it is worth more than a $100." "Why do you say that?" he asks. I retort, "Because there is a buried treasure on the property." "Oh, I didn't know that. I will then assess the value of the treasure and add it to the overall price of the land…and thank you for being so honest." I then replied, "No problem, honesty is the best policy."

Isn't that what we are supposed to do? But that is not what the parable tells us to do. It tells us to hide the treasure, and don't tell the guy. Is that right? If you go to the store to buy a refrigerator and the clerk rings you up for twenty dollars, wouldn't you say something?

"Sir, I think you may want to check that price again, I think you made a mistake." You would say something because it is the honest thing to do. Why does the parable suggest something that is dishonest? Jesus does not like buried treasure. For Jesus, if you are not going to use it to help someone, then give it to someone who will. Build the road.

I heard a story of a person who won a million dollars at a slot machine. Imagine sitting down on a random seat just at the right time and just at the right machine and pulling a lever that yields a million dollars. The person who won the prize had visions of providing a better education for the children, dreams of assisting the relatives and friends who are struggling in a bad economy, and had hopes of finally giving something substantial to a favorite charity: "At last I have the means to make a difference in the world." That is the kind of attitude you and I should have when God awards us with talent, skills, knowledge, or financial well-being. Whenever you are blessed, I want you to hear God say to you, "It's not for you. It is given to you so you can help people." What did we learn from the parable? God does not like money that is hidden away because buried fortunes cannot help people. If you have a surplus of goods, use it to build your road to salvation.

If God Asks You What You Want, Make Sure You Give Him the Right Answer

If God asked you, "What would you like me to do for you?" What would you tell Him? Do you have a ready-made answer on the tip of your tongue to give Him? That is what happened in the Gospel. Jesus asked James and John "What would you like me to do for you?" The two disciples asked for a truly godly gift. Not only do they want heaven, which, in itself, is a big prize, but they want the most important place in heaven: seats at the right and the left of the divine throne. Now before we all start to look down our noses at these two, remember the most important rule in fundraising: always aim high.

When I first came to St. Clement Shrine there were much needed repairs that required immediate attention. One of them was the padding on the kneelers. The old foam had packed down to the wood, and they had to be reupholstered. I had a kneeler campaign. People could donate $45 per kneeler. It was a successful fundraiser because it didn't require everyone to break the bank. After about a week, a gentleman called me and asked if there were any kneelers left. I said, "I think there are about thirty." He said, "I will take them all." Of course, I thanked him. I then told him that we had other "gift items" that needed filling such as the sound system. He paid for everything. So you see, always aim high. What went wrong with the two disciples? Why didn't they get their request? They failed to aim high enough. Is it possible that there is a higher request than the highest place in heaven? In fact, there is.

Immediately after this scene Jesus walked by a blind man and asked him the same question: "What do you want me to do for you?" The blind man said, "I want to see." Jesus honored his request, and the man began to follow Jesus. I have a question. What group is blatantly missing when Jesus dies on the cross? The mother of Jesus is there. The women who followed Jesus were there. Simon of Cyrene, who helped Jesus carry the cross, was there. The crowd was there, and the Sadducees and the high priest were there to satisfy their hate.

The Roman soldiers were in the front row. It seems every group in Jerusalem is represented except disciples. Where are James and John? Or rather, why are they not where they need to be. The reason is because they didn't answer the question correctly. The disciples should have answered Jesus' question with the same answer the blind man gave. They should have answered, "We want to see. We want to see so we can follow you. We want to see you turn the other cheek so we can follow you by doing the same thing. We want to see you stand strong before Pilate and not compromise the truth. We want to see you love your enemy and pray for your persecutors so that we can follow you. We want to see you forgive your enemies while you are on the cross."

Whenever you pray, make sure you get it right. Whenever Jesus asks you what would you like Him to do for you, make sure you aim high and give Him the best response? Tell Him you want to see so you can follow him. Jesus came as a road, a path to a better life. We have to take it.

While we are on the topic of James and John, I would like to ask the obvious question: if James and John do not get the place at the right and the left of Christ, then who does? Who possibly could be more worthy of the right and the left than the two Apostles? John and James have churches and cathedrals named after them. Who could be more deserving? Mother Teresa? John the Baptist? At the cross, where Christ wins redemption for all humankind, at the moment that has been anticipated by the prophets for the last thousand year, we are now able to see who the Father has chosen for the right and the left. There are two who are crucified with Jesus, one on his right and one on his left. Now we know who has the places of honor while Christ redeems the world: two unknown thugs, the lowest of the low. Why them? Why these two? What saintly martyr would not want to be at the Lord's side while he is on the cross?

I imagine heaven at the end of time. I can picture there are a group of people around St. Peter. St. Francis will have his followers, but there is going to be a mob scene around the two thugs, and I will be one of them. They represent us. We are all sinners who need God at the moment we are most vulnerable. Christ came for this reason: to offer us a way to salvation.

Conclusion

God is the perfect partner because he works with limited resources by choosing us. He can take a curse and turn it into a blessing and offers the roadmap for us to build a road to salvation. What better illustrates these attributes than the story of the Visitation in Luke's Gospel. Mary's cousin, Elizabeth, asks: "How is that the mother of my Lord should come to me"? I find the question to be a bit odd. If I were Elizabeth, I would have asked Mary a different question: "How did you know I was pregnant? I didn't tell anyone. In fact, I went into seclusion the moment I conceived. My husband didn't tell anyone because the angel Gabriel made him mute for not believing his words. He believes now. So how did you know I was expecting?" Elizabeth didn't ask the question that I thought needed to be asked. She asked a different question: "Why did the mother of my Lord come to me?"

Let's review. First, Elizabeth is supposed to be sterile, and she is too old to have a child. She is cursed. Now she is with child. So naturally, she is thrilled about that. God turned a curse into a blessing. Next, Elizabeth is happy because one of the prophecies of the angel came true. Elizabeth is also in the line of Aaron, the high priest. Not having a son would have been doubly shameful if she were not able to contribute to this important line. So John is not only a priest but a descendent of the high priest. In addition to this, Gabriel said that John would be a prophet. A prophet is someone who gives information from God to other people. When John leaped in his mother's womb, John was giving information to Elizabeth that she was in the presence of divinity. So naturally, Elizabeth is ecstatic to be in the presence of God and to have her son taking the role of prophet. Stack all these gifts into one moment, and you have Elizabeth thinking: Why is God so good to me? Mary answers her question when she proclaims her famous Magnificat. In this canticle, she explains to her cousin why God loves to exalt the humble. Elizabeth was humbled because she could not bear a child, likewise gives God an opportunity to surprise her with the gift of John the Baptist. So remember, whenever you are down, lowered, humbled, and deprived, that is a good place to be with God because God is most visible in the world when He lifts up the lowly.

If you are one of those who counts blessings each day—life, food, air, use of our hands, feet, and eyes; the forgiveness of God, the promise of heaven—then you can ask the same question that Elizabeth asked Mary: "Why is God so good to me"? Mary's song will always give you the answer: He raises up the lowly. It is precisely our flaws, our curses, and low status that offer God the opportunity to shine.

Partnership is a story. The wonderful narrative of the Incarnation would not be possible without God, but Mary and Elizabeth also played a role with their humility, patience, trust, prayerfulness, and righteous. If God is going to produce a story about us, then we need to have set skills in place. Let's take a look at the prerequisites needed for managing your partnership with God.

Part 2

You

Gabe de Guzman is one of the most impressive dancers I have ever seen. He does tricks with his body that no one else executes, in addition to flips, forward head springs, splits, bone-breaks, flairs, facials, head slides, and impossible holds. Needless to say, he is a lot of fun to watch. He is so explosive that his clothes take a beating. During a typical routine, his movements cause his hat or one of his shoes to be jettisoned, and his coattail is often flying somewhere above his head. He turned professional at the age of 10, and he started to choreograph major shows at the age of 16. The editors of "Dance Spirit" described him as one of the "Chosen Ones," an heir to the hip-hop throne (January 2014). In the article, Gabe offers three keys to success to boys who are just getting into the business: (1) ballet, (2) ballet, and (3) ballet. Why Ballet? Dance is not just about throwing your body around. It requires a rock hard core, balance, speed, upper and lower body strength, flexibility, endurance, grace, rhythm, agility, discipline, and team collaboration. Ballet provides the principal foundation that contributes to every type of physical demand put on a dancer. Athletes, actors, janitors, postal workers, and just about anyone can benefit from the discipline and grace of ballet. Gabe, a highly sought after hip-hop dancer and accomplished actor, owes his success to ballet.

Before we hit the dance floor with the divine, we need to have some of the basics in place. Otherwise, we will be stepping on God's toes and falling down a lot. The choreography will not look very elegant and beautiful unless we have discipline, grace, strength, and endurance. The question is not "how" we prepare ourselves but "where." The desert is the biblical location for advancing and solidifying a strong relationship with God. That is why Jesus starts his ministry by going into the desert. It is why the Israelites are instructed in the desert. There they learned how to listen to God, communicate, foster spiritual health, and depend on God for everything. These are all the essentials for partnering with God.

Josiah was eighteen years old when he became the acting king of Judea, just around the time Jeremiah the prophet started to warn the people about their relationship with God that apparently had chilled over the years. It was true. Josiah noticed that the chosen ones drifted away from God. They had other disturbing matters that occupied their minds, so the king decided to restore the Temple thinking that if the building looked nice, people would go back to church again. And so it began. While they were knocking down a few walls, someone found a very old book. They blew the dust off and gave it to the king. Scholars believe it was the book of Deuteronomy. The king read the text, and it forever changed the way he governed. The ancient manuscript represented the last words of advice from Moses before the people crossed over into the Promised Land. His instruction was simple: never forget what happened in the desert. Remember how you became close to God. Remember when you said to God, "We are in a desert and we don't have any water." Then God replied, "Well, hit the rock with your staff and water will spring forth." Remember when you didn't have any food, and God let food fall from the sky. Remember how you depended on God for everything, and how you bonded with God. The relationship was so special that God called you children. After Josiah read the book, he said, "We do not need to restore a building, we need to restore our hearts. We need to go back to the desert and get back what made us so special to God. We need to take back what we have lost over the passage of time." It often happens. We grow, we advance, we change. Yes, we make gains and accept losses as a result. But are we always better from the trade-off?

Back to Basics: Fresh Donuts and Great Coffee

When I was ten years old, my mother took me to help her do a few errands around town. Between the post office and the grocery store, we paid a visit to Dunkin Donuts. I ordered a plain donut. Why would a kid order a plain donut when the donut shop had the chocolate covered variety? Because a guy wearing a white apron and white flour all over his arms just came out of the kitchen and brought out a tray of plain donuts. I told the waitress that I would have one of those. I bit into the donut, and it was crunchy on the outside and still warm inside. It was delicious. The reason: it was just made. While I was in rapture, the waitress brought my mother a cup of coffee in a porcelain cup, which of course, is the proper way one should drink coffee. Before we left, she ended up with two free refills. Today if you go to Dunkin Donuts, the coffee is served in a paper cup, and if you anticipate needing a refill, then you will have to pay for a bigger paper cup, and the donuts are never crunchy on the outside and warm in the middle. I have nothing against the franchise. In fact, it is arguably one of the most flourishing businesses in the

US. Who could argue with such growth? Still, I miss the old Dunkin. Sometimes over the passage of time, and as we march forward on the road to success, we lose some of the qualities that made us special.

It is not the first time that I have missed a good thing in my past. When I advanced further academically in my Scripture studies at midlife, I acquired some extra poundage around the midriff. I began to have anxieties. I was always thin. Yet at fifty plus, the extra weight did not fill in my scrawny limbs, it, rather, went right to my stomach. I feared that the silhouette of my legs and hips would have the appearance of two sticks holding up a beach ball. I started to exercise, and to exercise discernment when it came to eating. I got back the body I once had. Life changes us, but that doesn't mean we cannot go back and reclaim the good that was lost over time.

Not long ago a taste test was conducted, and the majority of those who participated said that McDonald's coffee was better than Starbucks'. That news, of course, didn't go over very well with the folks at Starbucks. To remedy the situation, the owners closed all the shops nationally for three hours and taught all the employees how to make a cup of coffee. Apparently, over the passage of time, the old formula that made them famous was forgotten, and they needed to get it back again. It happens. Sometimes we lose a few qualities along the road of life. That does not mean that we cannot find what we lost. You may assert that you used to be always happy, you used to be generous with your time, you used to be compassionate and quick to help the unfortunate, you used to exercise, you used to pay attention to detail, you used to be close to your parents, you used to have more energy, you used to appreciate the outdoors and appreciate God in his creation, you used to be more carefree and didn't let the small stuff rattle you. If the present makes you sad in light of the past, then do what Josiah did. Go back and retrieve what was lost.

There was a guy who had a great idea, a phone, and a truck. Someone would call him and say, "I am moving to Florida, and I have all this nice furniture. I don't want to drag it all with me so, could you use it?" The guy with the phone and the truck would go to the house, take away the furniture and bring it to a family that couldn't afford such furnishings and even take away the old to make room for the new. It was such a simple yet brilliant idea that people started to throw money at the project. Cash has a way of changing things, and the idea grew into a fancy building with lavish offices and a sophisticated phone system. Someone who donated to this mission looked at the attention to its progress and success, and he said: "I think I liked it better when there was just a guy with a phone and a truck." Through the passage of time, we lose what made us special, and we have to get it back. Sometimes we have to return to when we first started to dream of greatness.

I encounter numerous medical students. I admire their determination and commitment. It is not an easy road. They tell me how they get through the sometimes grueling training. They dream. They dream about the people they are going to help. They dream about the people they will save, and the difference they will make. They dream, and that propels them to work with relentless determination so that someday they can live that dream. That is how it happened to me.

When I was about ten years old, I was in the car with Mom and Dad. We just left the church and on were on our way home. At that moment I made an important announcement. They were in the front seat, so I leaned forward and said, "Mom, Dad, I am going to be a priest." Dad didn't say anything. I am sure he didn't know what to think about the idea, so he just clutched his hands on the steering wheel and continued to drive the car. Mom turned around and said to me, "That's nice dear." She said it in one of those high pitched sing-song tones as if to say, "Tell me this twelve-years from now and your message will have more credibility." However, little did my parents know that while we were at church, I was dreaming. As I watched the priest on the altar, I started to dream that I was the one who would stand behind the pulpit proclaiming the Gospel. I would be the one to explain the Gospel in the homily without torturing everyone. I would be the one who would hold up the broken bread and say "Behold the Lamb of God." I would be the one making a difference in people's lives. I often go back to that moment in the car to remember the dream. That is why I often advise seasoned doctors and professionals to go back to their youth when they first started to dream and ask them, "Are you now living the dream?"

Yes, over time we change and need to address the erosion and wear and tear. The desert is not so bad. The Israelites often went to the Jordan desert during the cold rainy season of winter. If our relationship with God and neighbor has chilled, we need to seek a warmer climate. I know a lot of Bostonians who move to Florida for the winter. They return with a tan, a great smile, and sport no calluses on their hands from shoveling snow. They never have complaints. There are advantages to returning to where our ancestors began their monumental journey into the family of God. In the desert the Israelites learned to master four skills: (1) listening to God and his prophets (Moses), (2) communicating with God, (3) cultivating spiritual health, and (4) depending on God. I will take you through each one of the four because they make up the principle foundation of our partnership with God. Gabe, the hip-hop dancer, understands the contribution ballet has made to his success. So now we are about to train as ballerinas.

Chapter Five

Listen to God and His Prophets

In the last chapter the focus was on God and what God can do. Now the focus is on us. We need to be able to acquire simple but necessary skills to manage our collaboration with God. In the Gospel of John, two of John's disciples ask Jesus, "Where are you staying?" And Jesus invites them to come and see. They are about to discover that Jesus stays at the bosom of the Father because that is where he is from. We know this because the Gospel begins by telling us that Jesus comes from the bosom of the Father (John 1:18). So let us talk about what it means to be at the bosom.

The Secret to Success: Acquiring Privileged Information

Everyone who reclines at table in the ancient world gets a bosom buddy. Whenever you are in the reclined position and put your head back, it will rest on the chest or the bosom of the person beside you. While your head is leaning up against your bosom buddy, you will notice that your ear is only a few inches from the mouth of your neighbor. With the mouth of your companion so close to your ear, you will be able to hear everything, especially whispered secrets. When the Gospel says that Jesus is from the bosom of the Father it means that Jesus' ear is so close to the Father that he hears every-thing. Jesus knows what the Father says, what He is thinking, and what He feels. It is truly a privileged position to be so close to the

Father. One can know everything about the God. Once Christ knows everything about the Father, he is sent to us to give us the same information he received from the Father when he was at the bosom. It is almost as if we are also at the bosom of the Father when this information is shared with us. When Jesus is sent to us, Jesus tells us everything about the Father, what he says, what he thinks, and what he feels. The only reason why we can have such privileged information is that we are privileged, we like Christ are children of God.

To illustrate this great privilege, allow me to illustrate. One day my father stood on a flat rock in front of the Cape Cod Canal and made a cast. He caught a fish, and then another, and another. He discovered a crater, a depression at the bottom of the canal where fish gather to get out of the fast current. It is a resting hole. As the fish catch their breath, food passes overhead. It is sort of like sitting in your lounge chair during a football game and having your favorite snack food delivered to you on a conveyer belt. All the fish have to do is grab baitfish as they swim past. Well, my father found this hole. One day he took his friend, who was an outdoorsman, with him and showed him the rock and what happens when you stand on it and cast a line. The friend stood on the rock delivered a cast and caught a fish. Naturally, the friend was impressed. "Now, don't tell anyone about this place," my father warned him.

A week later, the friend is standing on the rock fishing. A guy, walking his dog, saw him and asked about the fishing. So the friend opens up his mouth and tells him everything about the rock, the resting hole, the great fishing spot. He did what my father told him precisely not to do. Now every time he goes to the canal to fish, there is a guy standing on his rock. So whenever my father finds a great place to fish, he tells only one person: me. Why? Because I am his closest friend; I am the son. Now when Jesus reveals privileged and secret information, to us, it means we are the Father's kids.

Here is another example. Dad arrived at the fishing club and saw everyone was sad because no one has caught a fish. So he goes out and catches a dozen trout. They all ask him what he is using. Dad told them the "white" fly. And they all said, "Oh, the 'white' fly." So for one day, all the members are very happy because they are catching fish. Why are they only happy for one day? Because the fish are not stupid; after a day, the trout learns that the white fly is a fake. So a week later Dad went back, and everyone was sad because the white fly was not working, and no one caught a fish. Dad went out and put on a different fly and caught another dozen. They all asked, "What are you using?" And Dad said, "The purple fly. Oh, the purple fly." So again all the friends are happy for one day. Naturally, Dad can't use the purple fly anymore because club members ruined it, so whenever he goes to the club, and he wants to catch a lot of fish he uses "the secret fly." There is only one other person besides my father who knows the secret fly, and that is me. I am his son. I have privileged information. The Father sent the Son precisely to give us privileged information. Knowledge that will help us do great things.

"Why Does God Hate Me": Maybe to Set Us Up to Achieve Great Things

I was in my sixth-grade gym class. It was floor hockey, boys against the girls. The teacher pulled me aside to ask if I would play on the girls' side to balance the teams. I reluctantly said, "Ya, I guess." Sure enough, there I was standing on the side with the girls and the guys made lots of comments on how I was a nice girl. I thought, "Oh no. What good can come from this? Why me? Why didn't my teacher pick another guy? Why does my teacher hate me?" I should mention that there was one other guy who played on the girl's team: my teacher who was a former goalie on his college hockey team. It was overtime and still no score. I told one of the girls to stand by the net. I got the puck and weaved my way past the boys toward the net. I passed the puck to the girl who was standing in front of the net. So she closed her eyes and took a swipe at the puck. She completely missed the puck. It bounced off of her foot and came back to me. So I flipped the puck in the net, and we won the game. Naturally, the teacher was really happy, all the girls loved me, and they each hugged me. Best of all, I crushed my foes, and I silenced the mockers. As I was basking in the glory—which does not happen too often in my life—I realized that my teacher set me up to be the hero. He knew that sixth-grade boys are not going to get the puck past a semi-pro. He knew that I was the only one capable of scoring a goal.

In the book of Deuteronomy, God tells the Israelites to heed his voice. Why did God tell them to listen? God was setting them up to do great things. Sometimes God asks us to do difficult things, and we think, "Oh no, why is he asking me to do something so hard? What good can come from this? Why does God hate me?"

Learn to Listen to the One's Who Know

I was on my way back from Home Depot with my friend Barry. We had a job at St. Clement and needed some material. I was driving on Route 93, and he said to me, "Take the next exit." I thought to myself, "I do not want to get off the highway. I will hit red light after red light, and it is rush hour. I won't get home for hours." So I pretended I didn't hear him. As we got close to the exit, my friend called out again, "You're going to miss it. Take the exit." So at the last second, I turned off. Now, why did I take the exit? Why did I go against my better judgment? Do I always cave into peer pressure? No, the reason I listened to him was because my friend is an ambulance driver. No one knows the roads around Boston better than an ambulance driver. Sure enough, he was right. We hit one light on the way back, and it was green. We were home in five minutes. I am really glad I to listened to him.

Remember when Jesus was talking to the crowd in John's Gospel? The crowd whined, "This talk is too hard for us. What good can come from this? Why does God hate us?" They walked away. Then Jesus turned to his disciples and asked them if they would leave him as well. Peter told Jesus, "Where else are we going to go. You have the words of everlasting life." That is the short answer. Here is the longer version.

Peter said, "Lord, remember when you told us to feed the crowd? We only had five loaves of bread and a few fish. I did the math and concluded that there was not enough food for everyone. You were right."

"Then there was the time when we went to Jairus's home. We went to her daughter's room, and you told the dead girl to get up. Everyone laughed at you. She was white as a sheet. She was dead, and she was not going to get up. You were right again."

You came on board just after I fished all night and told me to head for the deep for a catch. It was my professional opinion, as a commercial fisherman, that we were going to come up empty. I was at it all night, and if you can't catch fish at night when it is more opportune, then you are not going to do much in the day. I lowered the nets, and we nearly sank two boats with the fish. You were right. You are always right. That is why you have the words of everlasting life."

We may have a thousand reasons not to listen to the Lord. But we should always remember that there is one reason why we should: He is always right. And you will never go wrong if you listen to Him. So no matter how hard or difficult the request, just remember, He is setting you up to do great things.

The Prophets Who Speak for God Are Often the People Who Are Closest to Us

God talks to us and we need to listen, but often he uses the mouths of those who live near us. Here is an example. I took my first red-eye from Boston to California. I came back really sick, so it will also be my last red-eye. One of our seminarians was going to be ordained near Los Angeles, and he asked if I would give the homily at his first Mass. At the end of the Mass, the newly ordained stood up to thank his parents and gave them each a gift. He presented to his father a stole and said, "Dad, this is to remind you that the mercy, kindness, and generosity that I will offer in my ministry, I first learned from you. He then gave his mother a purificator. He told his mom, "When you finally leave this world and go to the pearly gates, St. Peter will ask you what you have you done in your life that should allow you to enter into heaven. This purificator will remind you to tell him that you lived your life in a way that inspired your son to be a priest." Needless to say, he didn't need me to give the homily. He just gave a powerful witness. Apparently, the parents passed on to their son everything he will need for his ministry.

One day I was with Dad. Gas prices were over four dollars a gallon, and the economy started to tank. I was concerned about all of this, and so Dad had to remind me that he grew up during the Great Depression. He told me this story. After it snowed, he went out to shovel driveways. He used the coal shovel which did not have a nice teflon coating, the kind which allows the snow to slide off the shovel. He had to kick the snow off with his feet or clean it with his hand after each use. It made the job labor intensive. After shoveling all day, he went into the living room and emptied out his pockets of the money he earned from clearing driveways of snow all day. He totaled his earnings, and then he stacked the coins in neat piles. He said he looked at the money and started to dream about what he could buy with the money. He didn't own his first bike until he was eighteen years old. Dad loved to fish as a boy so he had many hopes and the money would one day turn those dreams into reality. After the dreaming, he collected the money off the floor, walked into the kitchen, and gave it to his mother to buy food. My father then said this to me. "Never fear the hard times, Peter. They will make you strong and build character." My father had no idea that when he was young and handing his mother his hard-earned snow shoveling money, that he was building character that would one day inspire his future son to want to be a priest. Sometimes the prophets in our lives are the people that are closest to us. They give us information that will aid us, so listen to the prophets.

In the Bible, Job asks the question: "God, why are you so hard on us? And why do you make things so difficult? Maybe we are God's mouth. Perhaps we are supposed to deliver an important message to someone. God has great communication skills, and sometimes he uses prophets to deliver the message. We have to make sure we are listening.

Once You Have Valuable Information, Use It

Once I was on vacation, waiting in the parking lot for my confrère, Tom, to get back with lunch. While I was standing there, I watched a heavy-set man walking his chihuahua. The size mismatch between the two looked funny, but I didn't say anything. He came over to me and said, "How was the fishing." I said truthfully that I didn't do anything. He said, "Morris Island is loaded with fish. I was just there. I would be still there if I didn't have to go to work. The parking is a little tricky to find, but it is at the end of the road." When Tom got back, we left. Allow me to describe to you the public parking facilities at Morris Island. The parking lot is nestled in the midst of a very exclusive community. As you are driving there, you will see signs on both sides of the road that read "No Parking," "Tow Away Zone," "Keep Out," "We Hate You," "Leave Your Wallet at the Curb and Go Away." Tom suggested that we turn around. I said, "I am not giving up." As we started to think that we were not on the right road, I turn the corner and there is a big sign that reads: "Welcome Visitors." We pulled in and found a bunch of fishermen looking real happy. You could tell they had a great day of fishing. I went up to one of them and asked, "Where is everyone going?" He said, "The fish are gone because the tide changed." I was still determined not to give up. We walked about a mile and a half down the beach to the point, and it wasn't over. There were plenty of fish, and we had the whole place to ourselves.

Let me re-cap what happened. I got a valuable piece of information, and I left on a journey. During the course of the journey, I had bad directions and lousy advice. I got no encouragement, and I had many reasons to turn back. The only thing I had that persuaded me not to give up was a piece of information. That was all I needed. The lesson here is when you get some valuable information, do not give up on it.

Mary and Joseph acted in the same way when they got some valuable information. It was joyful news that God was going to send a savior into the world. After the information there were obstacles. Mary was pregnant outside of wedlock. There was talk of divorce. The child was born in poverty in a stable far from Mary's home. The baby's life was threatened by Herod who was one of the most ruthless and powerful men of the day. The threat was real, and they had to exile themselves to another country for an indefinite amount of time. They lost their child for three days, a nightmare for any parent. There were a lot of reasons to doubt, but Mary and Joseph never gave up because they had information. They never gave up, and as a result, the Scripture says that Jesus grew up in wisdom.

Where did Jesus get such wisdom? Where did he learn to eat dinner with tax collectors and sinners, forgive them, and give them all a second chance in life? He didn't learn that from the theologians and scholars in Jerusalem. He learned it at Nazareth. Where did Jesus learn to go to a synagogue during the Sabbath, meet a woman who was crippled for over eighteen years, and cure her? Not in the Temple. Where did Jesus learn to take off His outer garment, put a towel around His waist, and wash the feet of His disciples? He would never have learned that at the Temple. Where did Jesus learn to say on the cross: "Father forgive them for they know not what they are doing"? Not from the religious leaders. He learned it in Nazareth at the school of Joseph and Mary. Wisdom is the Word of God, and often we learn it through the voice of the prophets. Sometimes the prophets in our lives are the people who are closest to us. Remember to listen to the prophets.

Live the Message Before You Deliver the Message

God tells Elijah, the prophet, to go to Mount Horeb. Mount Horeb is in the middle of the hottest, and most brutal desert. It takes Elijah forty days to get there. Let's do the math. It takes one day to walk about twenty-five miles in the ancient world. Multiply that by forty, and that is one thousand miles. That would be like walking from Boston to St. Louis without any Pizza Huts, Holiday Inns, or Mini Marts along the way. This, of course, raises an important question. Why is God so difficult? Why meet on top of a mountain in the middle of a desert? Why not meet in, let's say, at the fifty-second floor of the Prudential building in Boston? For me, that would be a five-minute walk and one elevator ride to an air-conditioned restaurant. It would be so convenient, comfortable, and inviting. Why does God always have to be so hard? The reason is apparent when you read the story in the book of Kings. Elijah is going to deliver a message to the Israelites. He is to announce a long period of drought.

Before Elijah can deliver that message, he has to live the message. He experienced life in a barren place without water.

Let me give you another example. God tells Hosea to tell the people that his relationship with them is like "being married to an unfaithful wife." Hosea must have thought, "Oh no, this is not good." Sure enough, Hosea married an unfaithful wife, who lived like a prostitute. Hosea had to feel what God felt before he delivered the message.

One more example. God tells the prophet, Ezekiel, to alert the people of Judah that if they do not turn back to God, they will be taken into captivity. I can imagine Ezekiel's response. "Why can't I give the message you gave Isaiah to give, the one about the people eating rich foods and drinking choice wines? Why can't I have *that* message?" Sure enough, the Babylonians were a little upset with Jerusalem, and they took a few captives, Ezekiel among them, back to Babylon. In Babylon, Ezekiel warned the inhabitants in Jerusalem about their exile from Jerusalem. Anyway, the message was delivered. A prophet always lives the message before he delivers the message.

I went on a retreat shortly after I was ordained. The retreat director said, "So, Peter, how's it going?" I told him "I thought it was supposed to be easy." I then told him, "Several CCD teachers called in sick, and I had to put third graders in with the eighth graders. That was a disaster. The youth group got into the bingo balls and lost a few of them. Now I have the bingo committee mad at me. They teach you in the seminary about the ramifications of the hypostatic union. No one asks me about that. They didn't teach us anything about church boilers and why they always malfunction on Sunday morning." My retreat director patted me on the shoulder and said, "You're going to be fine."

Then he told me his own experience. He said, "I thought the day of my ordination was going to be the best day of my life. I was finally going to have a normal life. I would say Mass, preside over a few baptisms, and maybe meet a couple preparing for marriage. I expected a typical life of a priest, but that is not what I got. Instead, I was handed the envelope informing me of my first assignment. When I opened and read the formal document, I couldn't even pronounce the name of the place I was assigned to go. When I arrived, there were no roads, no running water, no church, and I didn't speak the language. For the first time in my life I felt truly alone."

"Twenty years later, I received a second envelope: my next assignment. On the day I left, I turned around to look at the place one last time. I saw roads, running water, a beautiful church, a vibrant faith, and many people crying because they did not want me to go. I turned to the Lord, and I said to Him, 'Twenty years ago I thought I was alone. Apparently, I was wrong. Look at the difference we made together.'" His story made me appreciate my hardships and struggles a little more. He was a prophet. He lived the message before he delivered the message to me.

Later that day we were at the liturgy, the same retreat director who just shared his story—a six foot plus, barrel-chested man—came over to me. I extended my hand to offer him the sign of peace, but he wrapped his big arms around me in a bear hug and said, "Peter, may the peace of Christ *disturb* you." I knew what he meant.

The Best Advertisement Is a Happy Costumer

Every year I go to the fly-fishing show. True, you can see the newest technology and the latest gizmos and gear. I go for the knowledge, not the toys. Every expert will be there, and I want to tap their brains. One year I went over to the fly-tying table of my friend. When I got there, he said he had not taken a break all day, and asked if I could watch the table while he got something to eat. I said, "Fine." So there I was, sitting behind this table, and a couple of guys stopped in front of the table. They started looking at all the things for sale on the table, and they point at a fly that had a lot of tinsel, in fact, it looked like a Christmas tree ornament. They asked what it was. I said, "That is the Goldie." Then I leveled with them, "Look, I am not a professional fly-tier. He will be back in a minute. I am also new to fly fishing, and I am not very good at it. In fact, you guys could out fish me any day, but even I can catch a fish with this fly. I don't know what it is—the gold, its flashy appearance, or the fact that it wiggles like a fish when you pull it through the water. Whatever it is, they always take this fly." One of the fishermen asked me if I knew how to tie one up. I said, "Oh, it is actually an easy fly to tie. That's the beauty of it. In fact, I'll show you." The guy said, "Can you wait for a second; I want to get someone." When my friend came back from his lunch, there was a crowd of people around his table buying his stuff. He said, "Where did everyone come from." I said, "I told them if I could catch fish with this fly then anyone could." It was my testimony. It was because I was not an expert that engaged them to listen. My friend sold a lot of flies and material that day because of his collaboration with me, a novice. That is why

Christ can call fisherman, tax collectors, zealots and other imperfect characters. Their witness and testimony are very compelling. Such people are God's best proof of his mercy, kindness, and generosity.

Scripture Is the Voice of God

In addition to prophets, another form of God's voice is Scripture. You read the Bible hoping to connect your life to God. Your instincts are well-formed. The Bible is ancient but not outdated. The application of old wisdom to contemporary issues, however, is not always easy. Biblical texts are filled with genealogies, wars, names of people and places that are hard to pronounce, details on how to sacrifice a variety of four-legged creatures, and terms that make no sense. In addition to these difficulties, the fresh and receptive ears that once heard the stories of the Bible, have, over the passage of time and repetition, been dulled by the effects of familiarity. Trying to tap inspiration and meaning out of the Bible is sometimes like picking blueberries from a bush that is planted in the middle of a bird sanctuary. If you flip through enough pages and skip over large sections of text like the prophetic oracles of doom, you may find "something."

I am now sixty-three years old and have spent my life praying with, reading, studying, preaching, and teaching the Bible. I have taken classes on Scripture in Rome, Princeton, Harvard University, Boston College, and have studied under some of the most renowned scholars in both Old and New Testament. I can honestly say that I rather read a book entitled *The Enigma of the Hebrew Verbal System* than go to a Red Sox game at Fenway Park. Yes, I am a Bible guy.

Scripture is not just a way of life or a resource for wisdom. For me it is food. As with anyone, the soul hungers for inspiration and the culture provides plenty of unhealthy means to add a little zip to life. Comfort food tastes good at first, but soon we feel bloated, weighed down, and tired. Healthy food gives us energy and motivation.

I went fishing once with Dad and his friend. After several hours in the sun, we took a break. Dad and I had some water, and our friend cracked open a beer. After I drank the water, I said, "I think I will go back out and fish." My father said, "I'll go with you." We then both turned to our friend and asked him he wanted to join us. He said he was tired and done for the day. I always assumed that if our friend chose the water over the beer, he would have caught more fish that day. Proper nutrition is essential for the spiritual life as well.

In the book of Proverbs, it says that Wisdom builds her house with seven pillars. Does that strike you as odd? It does because seven is an odd number. Most buildings have an even number of pillars. That is because buildings have balance and symmetry. When you have an odd number of pillars, one side of the building is going to be longer than the other side. So this raises a question. Why, then, does the house of Wisdom need an extension? Well, it tells us. The house of Wisdom needs the extra space for a bigger kitchen. Why does the kitchen need more room? Wisdom just invited everyone over for dinner. Wisdom wants to feed everyone's spirit, so we are all at our best. When I go to the hospital to be with a family who is grieving the loss of their loved one, I need to be at my best. When I go to Saint John's Seminary to teach a Scripture class so they will be able to inspire others with the word of God, I need to have my A-game. I need to continually feed the spirit because I cannot give what I don't have.

One day I was walking with my friend Fr. Jerry and we saw a potted bush out on someone's balcony. The plant was withered from top to bottom. Ironically, next to the pot was a watering can. I said to Jerry, "I think the dead bush is trying to say something. I can hear it speak, 'What good is a watering can if you are not going to use it.'" On the same note, we can ask to what advantage is having the Word of God if we are not going to listen.

Often we hear that people feel tired, weary, and drained of energy during the Christmas season. I think it is because spiritually we may be eating the wrong food. At this time of year, we are exposed to stimuli overload, and as a result, we get fatigued. Ironically, this is the time when we welcome the Word made flesh to be among us, a gift that should give us energy and inspiration. The shepherds saw the infant wrapped in swaddling clothes and left rejoicing. They didn't leave saying, "Boy, what an exhausting night this turned out to be."

Part of the reason we do not listen to God is that we are not properly connected to the divine. One spring day my father called and said, "Peter, the stripers are in the canal." To appreciate what my father said, let me tell you a little about stripers. They migrate, like birds, from the Carolinas to Nova Scotia every year in the spring. When they arrive at the Cape Cod Canal, they stop to get a quick bite to eat, and they go on their way. They don't hang out very long in the canal, so timing is crucial. So the way fishermen know that the stripers are in the canal is they first tell their wives "I'm taking the dog for a walk." Then you will see fishermen pacing up and down the Cape Cod Canal with a dog leash in one hand and a fishing pole in the other. You can always see the dogs shaking their heads wondering how long they are going to pace back and forth along the canal…as long as it takes for the fish to appear. When the fish finally arrive, the fishermen do not stop to call my father to tell him the good news. So how does my father know when the stripers are in the Canal? He lives sixty-miles away, and he doesn't even own a dog. He can tell when the lilacs are in bloom. It is certain proof every year. How do the lilacs know when the stripers are in the canal? Do they text each other? No, nature is connected.

A guy wrote a book on fly hatches—caddis hatches, mayfly hatches, stonefly hatches—I am sure you must have read the book. He claims that a fisherman can know when there is a hatch and certain bugs are coming off the water by observing the flowers. His point is this: all of nature is connected. Humans are an exception. We are usually out of the loop. Notice that animals are never hurt or killed during tsunamis. That is because they are connected. My point here is that humans are not connected with nature, and they are also not connected to God either. Here is an example from the story of the road to Emmaus.

Jesus told his disciples three times that He was going to suffer, be mocked, be crucified, die, and rise on the third day he would rise. You wonder by the reaction, if anyone was listening to Jesus that day. Jesus could not be clearer. Then, in fact, he goes to Jerusalem, he suffers, is crucified, and dies. On the third day, the women find the tomb empty. Not only that, but there were angels in the empty tomb who told the women that he rose from the dead. Yes, angels. Now let me ask, wouldn't you think that before the two disciples throw in the towel, abandoned their cause, and take off for Emmaus, that perhaps they would have stopped by the tomb to see if it was empty. Even if you had your doubts, wouldn't you walk a few blocks to check it out? Do you think they would have had a little curiosity about the news of the empty tomb? Perhaps the angels would still be there and would be happy to explain what happened. There is so much going on during the third day, wouldn't you want to stick around for a while to see what was happening? But no, they leave all the same. The reason they leave despite Jesus's prophecy, the reports of empty tombs and angels, and signs is because they are completely disconnected from God.

Do you ever feel down, disheartened, discouraged, not knowing why so many things are happening that are wrong? That is because we are disconnected from God. But look what happens to the two disciples on their way to Emmaus when they are reconnected with God. They have a sudden mood swing. They are full of hope, confidence, and willing to return to the story that God started with Christ. They have complete joy. So how do you get connected with God? What happened? The story tells us: the Scriptures: "Were not our hearts burning within us while he was talking to us on the road, while he was opening the Scriptures to us?"

I met someone who no longer felt any meaning in life. The person said, "I just run from one thing to the next, but no longer feel as if life has a particular purpose anymore. I asked the person, "When was the last time you felt your life had any meaning?" The person said, "When I used to go to church." I replied, "I have no further questions."

That is why we go to church. To hear the word of God. We spend all week listening to "other" voices and opinions and often it drains us. We go to church to hear the word of God and we get energized and recommitted. We have to remember that there are other voices that offer food that does not feed the spirit.

The parishioners at my first assignment insisted that the church offer the kids a place where they can go and get them off the inner city streets. I agreed, so we had a high school youth group. It quickly became very popular. Every year I had a "mystery bus adventure." The parents knew of course, but we always managed to keep the destination of the trip a secret from the kids. Usually, we went to Six Flags because it was always a sure bet. This one year I had the brilliant idea: to charter a boat and take the kids ocean fishing. I figured one day away from video games, the TV, and the computer. Getting in touch with nature would do them some good. After we got on the boat and the captain gave some instructions, we took off. Three of the kids immediately got sick. I take these same kids to Six Flags where they have rollercoasters that go up and down, Spiderman speed rides that twist your body inside and out, and elevator-shaft rides with a freefall, and the kids say, "That was cool, let's do it again!" They never get sick. But you put them on a boat with flat water at a speed of five-miles an hour and they get sick. How is that possible? We didn't even leave the harbor. So I asked the captain to turn back to the dock. One of the women chaperones said she would take them off the boat. So she made an announcement: "A few of the boys got sick, so I am taking them to the beach. I grew up in this area, and there is a lot to do. There is a boardwalk with ice cream shops, pizza parlors, video games, and rides. So, whoever wants to come, follow me." I thought, "Don't give that speech because they will all leave the boat." Sure enough, everyone walked off the boat except a few kids. I said to the captain, "Let's go fishing." It was a perfect day, the captain put us into fish, and the kids had a terrific time. They caught a lot of big fish, held them up for pictures, and the first mate filleted them so they could take their fish home already prepared for the grill. As we were coming into dock, the kids thanked me. They said, "This was the best day in their lives." I said, "Haven't you fished before?" They said that their parents were divorced and mom is always too busy working.

When we got on the bus, at the end of the day, none of the other kids who got off the boat came over to me and said, "This was the best day of my life." I didn't expect them to say that. Why? They can have the beach anytime they want. It is only ten minutes away from where they live. There are hundreds of pizza parlors and places to go shopping and stands to buy ice cream. They can play video games at home. This trip was once-in-a-lifetime chance to go out on a boat and catch some fish in the ocean, and they squandered the opportunity to do something that is available to them all the time.

Jesus said in the Gospel that his sheep listen to his voice. That doesn't mean there are no other voices out there, and there can be some pretty compelling voices. There is nothing wrong with going to a baseball game, but does Fenway Park offer eternal life? Does the shopping mall inspire you to get you through the darkest times of your life? I don't think so. Why do we follow Jesus' voice? He offers us things that no one else can offer or can give us.

Chapter Six

Communication

In the desert, the Israelites learned to talk to God. They saw their immediate needs, their desperate situation, first as slaves, and then as survivors in a desert. They had no other resources and no one else to turn. Their situation forced them to prayer. When we return to the desert, we are reminded that we need God just as much as the Israelites. We need to talk to God just as they did. In addition to listening, we need to have good communication skills with our divine partner. Scripture offers us numerous suggestions and helps. Here is a well-known passage from Matthew's Gospel on prayer:

And whenever you pray, do not be like the hypocrites; for they love to stand and pray in the synagogues and at the street corners, so that they may be seen by others. Truly I tell you, they have received their reward. But whenever you pray, go into your room and shut the door and pray to your Father who is in secret; and your Father who sees in secret will reward you.

"When you are praying, do not heap up empty phrases as the Gentiles do; for they think that they will be heard because of their many words. Do not be like them, for your Father knows what you need before you ask him.

"Pray then in this way:

Our Father in heaven,

hallowed be your name.

Your kingdom come.

Your will be done,

on earth as it is in heaven.

Give us this day our daily bread.

And forgive us our debts,

as we also have forgiven our debtors.

And do not bring us to the time of trial,

but rescue us from the evil one.

For if you forgive others their trespasses, your heavenly Father will also forgive you; but if you do not forgive others, neither will your Father forgive your trespasses.

If you ask St. Dominic how to pray, he will give you the rosary. If you ask St. Ignatius of Loyola how to pray, he will give you the Ignatian Spiritual Exercises. If you ask Mother Teresa, she will tell you to pray from the heart. If you go to a workshop on prayer, you may learn "centering prayer." I am glad someone had the foresight to ask Jesus how to pray. Answering this request, he gave us the Our Father. It takes seventeen seconds to pray. I timed it. That in itself is an important detail: it is short. In fact, all biblical prayers are short and for a good reason.

After the priest reads the Gospel at Mass, he gives a homily. He has four options: short and good, short and bad, long and good, long and bad. Take a wild guess which of the four is the most popular among the faithful in the pews? You are correct: short and good.

However, the people at church never get experience this. So what do you think is the second most popular choice of the four? It is short and bad. So knowing that statistic, let me ask you a question? When you turn to God in prayer, do you think God favors long and bad? Do you sense that He wants us to babble on and on? My assumption, at least according to the cited passage above, is no. So the Lord gives us a prayer that is short and good.

It is good because everything God wants to hear from our lips is in that prayer. When we pray the Our Father, we tell God that we are so close to him that he is like a father to us. God likes to hear that. When we say the Our Father, we tell God that we depend on him for everything, even the most common and simplest thing like a piece of bread. God likes to hear this. When we say the Our Father, we tell God that no matter what is going on in our lives, we want his will to be done. God likes this. When we say the Our Father, we tell him we appreciate his mercy and forgiveness so much that we are always willing to offer the same kind of mercy to others. God likes to hear this. When we say the Our Father, we ask God to take away any evil so we will never hurt him through sin. God likes this also. As I said, the Our Father has everything God wants to hear from us.

Jesus often prayed during his time on earth. What do you think he prayed? Of course, the Our Father. When Jesus went into the desert for forty days and nights and was tempted by the devil, what prayer did Jesus say? The Our Father: "lead us not into temptation but deliver us from evil." When Jesus was in the wilderness, and he wanted to feed the five thousand, rather than send them away, he took the only available food, a few loaves of bread. He looked up to heaven to pray. What prayer did he use? The Our Father: "Give us this day our daily bread." When Jesus was in the garden before his arrest, the Scriptures say that Jesus prayed. What was Jesus' prayer? Again, the Our Father: "Your will be done." When Jesus was on the cross before he died, he turned to his father in prayer. What prayer was on Jesus' lips? The Our Father: "as we forgive those who trespass against us." The Our Father is the perfect prayer for us as well.

Words Are Often Short, the Conversation Can Be Brief, But Know that a Relationship Takes a Lifetime

When I was in high school, I would go to work with my father on the weekends. As we were on route to the job, Dad would often reveal to me what it was like growing up during the Great Depression. Once he told me that when he was a kid the family was going to be evicted from their apartment. Around that same time, a bank was auctioning off a house. Some builders wanted to buy the house and flip it. That is, they would make repairs, add embellishments, and re-sell it for a higher price. It was apparent from the get-go that the Grover family had no chance at getting that house. Dad said, "My father left at noon to go to the auction with his lawyer, while Mom went into the room to pray. About twenty minutes later my mother came out of the room and said, 'We got the house.' I asked her how she knew because Dad was still at the auction. 'I know,' she said, 'because I prayed.'"

I interrupted my father's story and asked, "What happened?" Dad told me, "We got the house. Your grandfather was the only one who showed up at the auction." Dad assured me that this was not the only time that "Ma prayed for the impossible and got it." Naturally, after hearing that story, I wanted to get the advice of an expert at prayer. I needed to know why God always answers her prayers. So I went over to my grandmother's house and asked her how she prays. Now pay attention to this because this is important. She said, "I pray the Our Father, but with this detail: I pray it all the time." She said, "Peter, there will be times in your life that God will ask you to do something you do not want to do. Pray the Our Father, and mean it: 'your will be done.' There will be times when you do not know where the next meal will come from, pray the Our Father, and mean it: 'Give us our daily bread.' There will be times when people will hurt and disappoint you, pray the Our Father, and mean it: 'As I forgive those who trespass against me.' If you pray it all the time and mean it, your prayer will be heard. The Our Father may take only seventeen seconds to pray, but it represents a lifelong commitment.

If You Are Going to Pray, Then Imitate the Experts

I know a shorter prayer that is just as powerful. It is only one word: Wow! I know this prayer is not found in the devotional prayer books, but it is in the Bible. In Psalm 8 it says that the glory of God will be chanted and praised from the mouth of babies and infants. What? How do babies and infants become experts at prayer? The reason: they are seeing things for the first time. Did you ever see young children when they taste chocolate for the first time? Their eyes get wide. It is a lot of fun to witness. Did you ever see a baby's face when he or she sees a frog for the first time? Dad seats the child on the ground and show them the frog and say, "See the froggy. Do you want to see the froggy jump?" Their eyes widen, they open their mouths, and some inarticulate sound comes out. "Ahhhh." Please know that when that child opens his or her mouth and makes that sound, God is in heaven saying: "Finally, someone notices me." God loves that prayer. Here is the question we need to ask ourselves when we pray. Do we notice God in our lives? That is how we know that we are praying like the experts (i.e., infants).

Remember Simeon. He was in the Temple area when he held the child in his "bent arms." He prayed "Now I have seen salvation." He held a baby and saw his savior. He opened his mouth and since then, everyone who prayers Night Prayer in the Liturgy of the Hours every night before they go to bed repeats what was said. I modify the prayer a bit. "I saw you today." "I witnessed your terrific work today." "I appreciate what you did for me today." If you pray like that, then you are a pro.

That is exactly what happened to the shepherds when they saw their Lord laying in a manger. They saw God in a baby. To illustrate, let me tell you my version of the Christmas story. God sent the angels to the philosophers, and the angels said: "Behold the sign, an infant wrapped in swaddling clothes and lying in a manger." So the philosophers went out and saw the child and said, "It is metaphysically impossible that this newborn is God. We all know that God is infinite. God has no beginning or end. God cannot be born of a woman." And they went away unimpressed. Then the angels appeared to the scientists, and they went out and saw the child wrapped in swaddling clothes and said, "This cannot be a divine event. It is biologically impossible for a virgin to give birth to a child. We call this a myth." And they went away unimpressed. Then the angels appeared before the social workers, and they went and saw the infant lying in the manger. They say, "It is impossible that this child is to be the savior of the world. He will never have the money or the education to make an impact on the world." And they went away unimpressed. Then the angels went to the shepherds. They saw, and they rejoiced. So I pulled one of the shepherds aside, and I said to him, "Hold it; why are you so happy?" He said, "Because we have seen the savior of the world." I said, "The philosophers, the scientists, and the social workers said it is impossible. How is it that you know?" The shepherd replied, "Why of course this child is God. God loves doing the impossible. You just have to have the eyes to see it."

Do you have shepherd eyes? Do you believe that anything is possible with God? Do you say that in prayer? Then you are an expert because you have shepherd eyes. If you want to pray well, then you need to see God in your life.

At a seminarian scholarship dinner, the hosts of the event offered a silent auction. One of the items on the floor was "A Day of Fly Fishing with Fr. Peter." The highest bidder was a generous state senator. He called me and wanted to claim the prize. I asked him where he wanted to go. He told me somewhere local, so he would not have to travel far. I said, "Boston Harbor is loaded with fish this time of year." He met me at the church, and I drove him to a place with plenty of parking. After we put on our waders and rigged up the fly rods, we took a walk along a beach until we came to a point where the harbor and the ocean met. I told him, "This is a great place to fish." We had the whole place to ourselves. I like the location because there is always a strong current of water flowing due to the tide change. Fish are like people. As I mentioned earlier, they want to recline on a La-Z-boy and have their food served to them. The big fish lay behind a rock or depression in the sand and watch all the food pass by them in the current: shrimp, baby bunkers, soft-shell crabs, lobster tails, etc. You simply flip your fly into the current and let it drift, and if there is a fish waiting, you are going to have a good fight on your hands. So I gave him a fly and told him I was going to check out some water around the bend. I figured I better look like I am working hard for my client. When I came back, I was happy to see that the senator was fighting a fish. I put him in a good spot. When I got to him, he looked particularly happy. He released the fish, and we stood there in silence, taking in the beautiful sunset over the skyline of Boston. He said to me, "I really needed this today; there is so much stress where I work." I told him that we were only ten minutes away from his office (two hours away in traffic), and he could enjoy the beauty of God anytime he needed. It is always here, but we don't make the time to enjoy God's creation.

A year later I bumped into the senator's friend, and I asked him how the elected official was doing. "Oh," he said, "great! He quit his job and bought a boat."

One sure way to appreciate God is through the work of his hands. That is why I fly fish. When I catch a beautiful brook trout, I say to God, "You did a nice job with this one." God wants to be noticed. One word can say it all, "Wow." We have to notice God in our lives if we are going to be good communicators with God.

Remember the parable in Luke's Gospel of the rich man and Lazarus? It is a sad story because the rich man is tormented in flames. We learn from the story that the tragedy was easily preventable.

What did the rich man do wrong? He didn't have Lazarus beaten and thrown in jail for trespassing. He did not ridicule him, demanding that he get a job and work for a living like everyone else. What did the rich man do wrong? I think I know what happened. I suspect that the rich man did not notice that there was a poor man at his doorstep who needed some scraps that fell from his table. The rich man probably had a lot on his mind. He was entertaining guests at his banquet; he has to be apprehensive about the plummeting prices of olive oil in Jerusalem, be concerned whether his stocks were going to up, worried about the work ethic of his employees, anxious about the security of his wealth. I conclude that the rich man didn't even notice that there was a man at his gate. I presume that he was so caught up in his own world that he didn't even see Lazarus or understand his need. It happens. We get so caught up in our world, our problems, and our challenges that it is easy to miss the most essential thing in our life.

Communication leads to Opportunity

Let me retell the story in a way that the parable will have a happy ending. So I imagine that I am a rich man and I die. I wake up in heaven the angels are chanting praises, the saints are applauding, and father Abraham is greeting me with both arms in the air. I say to Abraham, "Timeout, hold it for a second. Why is everyone so happy that I am here?" I thought you guys do not like rich people. Then Abraham says to me, "Do you remember the time you held a banquet and after you all ate sumptuously, you got into your thousand-dollar suit and went out the door to go to a meeting." I said, "I vaguely remember but go on." "As you were leaving your mansion on your business trip, you noticed a poor guy was sitting outside your door. He had sores all over his body." "I'm still following you," I said. Abraham continues, "You turned to him and asked, 'Can I help you, sir?' He told you he was very hungry and wanted you to give him a few scraps that fell from your table. You mumbled something under your breath and marched into the house. Ten minutes later you came out and handed him a platter full of food. The poor man, said, 'Lobster tails, I love lobster tails. You wouldn't happen to have some melted butter?'" I said to Abraham. "That is it? The reason I am in heaven is that I gave a guy some leftovers?" Abraham said, "No that is not the reason you are here. The reason you are here is because you used to do it all the time. You noticed the needs of people. You noticed when God's closest friends were in need." And you noticed all the time. Part of a successful relationship with God requires communication, but communication is only as good as our ability to notice God in our life, as well as noticing opportunity.

So we have to be good at noticing God in our lives. Here is an example. One time the Visa people put a stop on my church credit card because somebody was trying to use it to buy Rhode Island. I was on hold waiting for a human to answer so I could figure out what was going on. The doorbell rang, and my office manager said there was a guy who wanted to see me. I had to discontinue my phone call. I opened the door, and a gentleman is standing there, who was about my age, said, "Peter, it is so good to see you again. My name is Duker."

I have a question for you. How many people do you know in your life by the name Duker? I know only one person with that name. He was my friend when I was twelve years old. I haven't seen him in over forty years. When I recognized him, I felt as if I was whisked back to my childhood. In a rapid exchange of information, I learned that he married the girl I wanted to marry when I was twelve. He informed me that his kids are big Celtics fans and while they were at the game, he decided to look me up. Why am I reporting this to you? That night I took out my large monthly calendar, and I wrote in the square which marked the date when this meeting took place: "Duker came to visit me today." Before I go to sleep, I always write down all the extraordinary things that happen to me that day. Once I wrote that Dad called me saying that he was accepted into an exclusive fly-fishing trout club and that I could fish anytime I wanted. I wrote that down. My mother called me once telling me that her long therapy had come to an end and she was finally leaving the nursing home to go back home. I wrote that down. I wrote down the day I was accepted to the doctoral program at Boston College. Sometimes the day goes by so fast that we forget to savor the special moments that took place.

I was in my office one day and Carol, our office manager, asked me what I did with a marriage certificate. I panicked because I know you cannot make errors with government documents. She said, "Think for a minute." So I said, "I remember sitting at my desk, and you gave me the certificate to sign. Then you gave me a pen. Then I remember signing the certificate and then...and then... I gave it back to you." At that moment Carol was looking in the file and found it. "Yes," she said, "you are off the hook." At that moment I raised my hands in the air with a sigh of relief, and I announced:

"For once, I didn't mess up." We sat there for at least a minute laughing. So that night before I went to bed, as it is my practice, I went back over the day to remember all the little things that happened, the things that go by unnoticed because we get so busy with "stuff." I remembered that fun moment in the office. I always end my day praying with that one word: "Wow." I go to sleep knowing that I noticed and appreciated God this day. And if I ever have any doubts that God is not crazy about me, that he is not watching out for me, and keeping me in his plans, then all I have to do is take out my calendar, flip through the pages that represent the blessings of my life, and all the doubts just go away.

Chapter Seven
Healing

The Israelites found healing in the desert. If we want to have a strong partnership with God, we need to be spiritually healthy, able to love without limits. We must be free from guilt, scrupulosity, fear, anxiety, father wounds, and grudges. The problem is that we either live unhealthy lives, trying to feed ourselves with food that does not give us the right energy and motivation, or we do not heal when we are wounded. Sure, we get beat up in life, but we need to be able to heal quickly. This chapter will discuss how we can heal if we have been wronged, and also how to live a life that will allow us to maintain a healthy spirit. It is our responsibility to listen, communicate, and maintain a healthy spiritual life.

Let's Turn to the Experts on Healing

The Gospels report that there was a woman who was bleeding for twelve years. She thought, "If I can only touch the hem of his garment, I will be cured." There is, of course, a problem.

The problem is this: Jesus is in a hurry. Jairus's daughter is on the brink of death, and the clock is ticking. He has to get there before she dies. I would even say that this is one of the most significant of Jesus' miracles. Turning water into wine may be nice to party patrons, but saving a little girl is the kind of sign that could appeal to modern sensibilities and restore belief in the divine.

Understanding the risks, the woman also knows that this is her last resort, her only hope. She will not necessarily jeopardize the life of a little girl if she surreptitiously reaches down to touch the hem of his garment. It worked. She is immediately cured. As soon as she finds out she is healthy, Jesus stops his emergency run to the little girl. The Lord, who seemed to be in a hurry, now has all the time in the world. Jesus asks, "Who touched me?" The disciples are in a state of incredulity. "What are you talking about? Look at the crowd that presses in on you; everyone is bumping into you. We have a serious crisis; there is a girl that is dying; keep focused; you are distracted. Jesus doesn't budge, and he won't until someone comes forward.

The woman is busted. She anticipates a reprimand and humiliation. Her illness will be exposed, and she will probably get blamed for the child's death. She is not the only one who is about to have a panic attack. Every tick of the clock is precious to the synagogue leader. Confronting this woman is going to take away precious seconds. Yet, Jesus wants to hear her story and appears to have all the time in the world. Every second that Jesus needs to hear her account is time well spent. So the woman tells about the twelve years of suffering, the doctors' inabilities, and the money spent. This monologue will take some time. I know because my father is a senior and every time I ask one of his friends how they are doing, I know I am going to get the latest colonoscopy report, and it is never short. Jesus gets the entire story. Then Jesus tells her "Go, your faith has saved you." She is no longer a social outcast, no longer unclean, no longer in pain, liberated from the expensive and complex healthcare industry, and she gets her life back. Healing involves a lot of factors, each as important as the other. She needed to make some critical decisions, take risks, and believe in the Lord. Healing resulted in a number of moves with a strong attitude, and she did what she needed to do to get well.

The Lord Is the Model of Healing

It takes time to heal. We hear this often when we talk to medical personnel. Sometimes it takes years to heal, especially for victims of abuse. When people suffer a family tragedy, lose a loved one due to separation or death, or encounter rejection, I tell them that their most important job for the moment is to heal. They need to do everything they can that will encourage healing: rest, healthy food, exercise, prayer, forgiveness, time with friends, cultivate interests, etc. We need to do all of the things that can help us regain our strength, self-confidence, and empathy toward others. The perfect model for healing is Christ himself. He suffered every physical and psychological affliction. Yet he healed. I believe he appeared to us after his death to show us precisely how to heal. Here is the story retold of Jesus appearance to the disciples after his death. Keep in mind how Jesus manifests himself as a healed friend.

Jesus tells the disciples to cast the net and they will find something. So the disciples catch 153 very large fish. It is a rather odd number, and Scripture scholars have scratched their heads for years trying to figure out the meaning of the figure. If you ask a fisherman what the significance of 153 fish might be, you will hear him say it means you are having a really good day.

I was engaged in a conversation about fishing one day with my father and a friend. The friend turned to me and stated, "Oh, by the way; happy birthday, Peter." Dad heard him say that and asked me, "When was your birthday." "Last week," I said. Dad felt bad that he completely forgot my birthday. Anyway, we continued to talk about fishing, and Dad told the story about a steelhead he caught in the Salmon River thirty years ago. Naturally, he recalled every detail. You see, fisherman can forget birthdays, but they never forget a big fish.

I had a similar experience. Thirty plus years ago I was ordained. It is supposed to be the most special day in a priest's life, an event he will remember for the rest of his life. Actually my ordination is a blur. I do not remember who was there, what the bishop said, or what I was wearing. Three days after my ordination, I took a few days with Dad, and we went fishing. I caught two large steelhead trout. I still remember every detail of that day. I can point exactly to where I was standing in the river, what I used, and what I was wearing.

So I suggest that the 153 very large fish implies that the disciples were having a great day. But there is more. They are having breakfast on the beach with a charcoal fire (which, by the way, is illegal in Massachusetts). There is still more. They are joined by their best friend who was dead and buried a week ago. Just when you think it doesn't get any better than that, Jesus tells Peter that he is the shepherd of the church which means he has been declared a bishop. Not a bad promotion.

So we know that Peter and the other disciples are having a good day. But my question is this: Why is the Lord so happy? Why is Jesus dishing out such gifts and promotions? Shouldn't Jesus be angry? The disciples walked out on him less than a week ago. Wouldn't one think that Jesus should be holding a grudge? Perhaps feeling sorry for himself? Why shouldn't he be brooding over his injuries and seeking revenge on his opponents, betrayers, accusers, and torturers?

No, Jesus doesn't seem to be angry at all. Why? Jesus is healed, completely. We sometimes overlook this fact when we recall to memory the Resurrection? Think about it. No grudges, no anger, no lingering wounds that need immediate attention. So my next question is this: How did Jesus heal so quickly from the trauma of the cross? The reason is this. Jesus has a system in place that allows him to heal quickly. He is well connected with his Father in heaven, he forgives, and he is generous. He has all the conditions in place in his life to heal fast. Healing is a multi-part operation.

After Jesus died, after he bowed his head and gave up his Spirit on the cross, the Gospel of John reports that Jesus returned to the Father. In John's Gospel, Jesus came from the bosom of the Father. As I mentioned above, the term "bosom" is an ancient expression which highlights the seating arrangement when two or more are reclining at table to eat. So when Jesus returned to the bosom of the Father, I imagine that he was with him at dinner. I am speculating of course, but I can picture the scene. The Father raised his glass and proposed a toast: "To my Son who just saved the world." Jesus heals quickly because of his strong relationship with his Father, which he fosters by prayer, generosity, forgiveness toward others, and trust in the divine plan.

There Are a Number of Requirements that Are Needed to Heal. Leave One of Them Out, and You Will Compromise Your Success

My formula for staying physically healthy is simple: get plenty of rest, breath clean air, eat well, exercise, and don't do drugs. What is the first thing the hospital staff does when someone is admitted to the hospital? They connect an I.V. machine to the patient with a loud alarm and place it within inches of the patient's ears so the person can never get any rest. That is because every five minutes the alarm clock on the machine goes off and no one rushes into the room to turn it off. Then they lock all the windows shut which assures that all the illnesses and diseases remain in the room. They serve hospital food. Then they strap the patient to the bed so he or she cannot exercise, and then they pump the patient with drugs.

I was at the hospital with a family. I started the prayers, and like clockwork, the I.V. alarm went off. It was loud, so people were having a hard time hearing what I was saying. The nurse didn't come in to silence the alarm, so I went to inform the staff. When I found the patient's nurse I told her my philosophy on health care. I unleashed seventeen years of pent-up conviction that hospitals do not promote healing the way they should. After my rant, I figured this nurse would never like me again. She surprised me by telling me that I was right. She said, "You do not begin to heal until you return home."

The nurse is correct, but why? Why is it that we heal at home? It is because of God. God gives us everything we need in our bodies to heal. The doctor does not heal the broken bone; the body heals the broken bone. God made our bodies and our spirits to take a few bumps along the way. For example, you break a leg and get it set. Then you do not use the leg. While you are not using the leg, you get plenty of rest, breath some fresh air, and eat good food. Add therapy, and you are back running marathons before you know it. God knows that we get bruised and banged up in life. That is why he gave our bodies the ability to heal if we do the things we need to do. Jesus once said to turn the other cheek. Insults, under appreciation, being ignored, public humiliation are all forms of slaps in the face. Jesus told us to turn the other cheek because we have to remember that a slap in the face is just a slap in the face. Such experiences do not require a trip to the Emergency Room, surgery, or prolonged treatments. They hurt, but if treated, one heals quickly. Forgiving, cutting someone slack, giving someone a break, mending a relationship, having patience, and giving constructive instruction all contribute to a speedy recovery from a slap in the face. One of the fastest cures for me is the pull-up. If you cannot do pull-ups, push-ups will work just as fine. If you have kids, a wife, sensitive folks nearby, you will want to have a gentle spirit. Pull-ups will give you a gentle spirit. We need to do the things that allow us to heal while not endangering others to injury.

St. Paul asked the Lord three times to take away the "thorn" in his flesh. To this day, no one knows what he meant by the metaphor: a toothache, the Galatians, his mother-in-law. Paul does tell us what the Lord told him: "My grace is sufficient." That means that God gives us what we need when we need it.

In life, we get hurt, sometimes crushed. We need to heal. But sometimes we live as if we were a patient in a hospital, strapping ourselves to a bed of inactivity, drugs, not eating well, not doing the healthy things we need to do to win back our spiritual vibrancy. "My grace is sufficient" means that God has given us everything we need to keep healthy or to heal when we get hurt. We have to use the gifts.

Education Is Expensive and Painful, But It Will Give You a Higher Payout

I had a little carpentry business before I entered the seminary. I got a call from a guy who wanted the second floor of his house finished. I asked him what he wanted me to do for him. He said, "Just the bare basics: sheetrock and hollow core doors." I wrote up a contract. He liked the price and signed it. As I got started with the job he came to me and asked, "Do you think I should insulate the walls?" I told him it would be a lot harder to insulate after the sheetrock is up. He said, "Do it." Then he said, "Now that the walls have nice soundproofing, it would be wrong to put in hollow core doors. You better put in solid doors." Then he wanted ceiling fans, a walk-in closet, and stated: "That is not enough shelving. Kids have a lot of toys. Add some shelves, and while you are at it, you may as well paint the joint." I was happy to get the extra work. He was pleased with the job when I finished, and so I sent him a bill. In addition to the original contract, I sent him an invoice for the extras. A few days later he informed me that he would pay the agreed amount that he originally signed, but he would not pay for the extras. No paperwork, no money. If I didn't like it, then I can call his cousin, the lawyer.

I was devastated. Before the call I was happy and on top of the world doing what I loved. After the call I hated my job, and worse, I lost all my confidence. I needed to get my energy and enthusiastic stride back that I lost. I needed a rope to pull myself out of the dark hole. I called Dad.

He told me that I learned something about running a business that would have cost me a lot more if I went to school. When I hung up the phone, I did what I needed to do to heal. I forgave the debt. Why? Did I do it because I am a nice guy? I wish that were true. Did I do it because I felt bad for the man who had two little kids and was struggling with finances? No. I forgave him for purely selfish reasons. I needed to heal. I needed to get my life back to where it was before the crisis, and forgiveness was the main ingredient.

I have an invisible sign over my desk. No one sees it, but I look at it whenever I have a setback. It reads: "Feel used, hurt, betrayed? Then it is time to go fly-fishing." I go out in the middle of God's creation, stand in a river, and see beautiful trout, and all the sunshine and peace return to my soul. If I stay connected with God then I know I will be fine no matter the crisis.

Anger Is a Good Resource, So Use It

Anger is a good emotion because it ensures health. God gave us anger to help us identify problems. Anger also gives us the energy to fix problems. When the dog is chewing on your brand new shoe, you are not going to sit on the recliner and eat ice cream. In haste, you are going to stop the dog from destroying your property. Explosive energy gets things done. Anger alerts us to problems, so whenever I get angry, I say, "No problem," because I am pretty good at fixing problems. If I can't fix the problem—which is rare—then I will sit on the recliner and eat ice cream. So to recapitulate, anger helps us to solve problems. Some folks, however, are not good at solving problems. Instead of putting their energy into solutions, they create a drama. Drama includes victims, persecutors, and rescuers. If you are ever swept into someone's drama when they get mad, be prepared to switch roles. First, you will be identified as the persecutor, then you will feel guilty or sad, which turns you into a victim. You will also feel the need to rescue the person who initiated the drama.

The one who creates the drama usually begins with the role of the victim. Of course, every victim has a persecutor. After the persecutor is persecuted by the victim, the victim sees the harm inflicted on the said persecutor and then turns into the rescuer. Drama can get complicated. By the end of the drama, everyone involved becomes a victim, persecutor, and rescuer—all this without really solving the problem. This is why television sitcoms are entertaining. They illustrate personalities that cannot solve problems. Instead they create a drama.

Here is my advice: stay out of other people's drama when they get upset and cannot use the anger to fix the problem. You can love them and try to help them, but do not be cast in the soap opera. If you can avoid dramas in your life, you will experience lower stress, sleep better at night, and avoid eating too much ice cream. Use anger properly to your advantage, and you will stay spiritually healthy. Remember, everything breaks, things go wrong, and people disappoint. Anger is a good alert but we need to focus on fixing, not magnifying problems.

Sometimes Healing Comes from the Kindness of Others

Let me ask this. Why did the Lord send out the Apostles in twos without any food or money? Imagine traveling without a few dollars for the tolls or something to eat on the way. That doesn't make any sense. The Lord sent them out with nothing perhaps because the disciples are not going to need it. They have been empowered to cure the sick, cast out demons, and deliver a hopeful message. Let me explain why they will not need anything when they have possession of such extraordinary powers.

I fell and broke my thumb. I was going to ignore the pain, but that night there appeared to be a golf ball lodged in my thumb. I went to the emergency room. It cost me 75 dollars to register as a first-time visitor, 150 dollars for the nurse to take my temperature, 300 dollars for the x-ray, and 300 dollars for the doctor to tell me that my thumb was broken. I said, "I know it is broken, that is why I am here." He said, "Unfortunately, there is not much we can do with it." I wish he told me that when I first came in the emergency room. I would have taken my money to the North End of Boston and had a very nice dinner.

Now to my point. Let's suppose I was on my way to the emergency room and I ran into the two disciples that Jesus just sent out in twos. I wave to the two disciples, and one of them says, "What happened to your thumb?" I tell him that I think I broke it, and I am on my way to check it out at the emergency room. He said, "Let me see that." So he touched it and cured me. Do you think I am not going to be grateful? Think of the money he saved me, not to mention five hours of waiting in the emergency room? Do you not think that I am going to ask him, "Can I buy you lunch?" Or, "Do you have a place to stay for the night?" Or look at his feet and say, "Can I buy you a pair of shoes?" What is the message here? If you put your gifts in the service of God, like the disciples' gift of healing, and you use your gift to help others, you will not have to worry about anything. We heal each other by what God has given us. If we want to heal we also have to know how to be healed.

Even the Biblical Poster Boy For Anxiety Has a Reason Not to Worry

One of the unhealthiest situations we can encounter is high stress. It is not good for our heart and blood pressure, it is not good for our sleep, and it affects our relationships. If we want to live a healthy life, we need to manage our stress. The Bible often addresses this. Jesus said do not worry about what we are to eat or what we are to wear or worry about our own very lives. Sound advice, but I have a question: Who in the Bible is the poster boy for anxiety? If anyone should be worried about what he is to wear or about his very life, who would it be? Answer: the man who fell to robbers in Jesus parable of the good Samaritan. Jesus tells the story of a man walking from Jerusalem to Jericho. He fell to robbers, they stripped him of his clothes, beat him, and left him half dead in a gutter. Maybe this man should be an exception to Jesus' anxiety rule. Maybe he should be worried. And here is why. Jesus tells us that two priests pass by without giving the man assistance. If a priest and Levite, the most spiritually mature class in society, pass by the man without helping him, then maybe he is in deep trouble. Maybe he should be worried.

Do Jesus' words "Do not worry" apply to the man who fell to robbers? What reassurance can Jesus give the man to persuade him that he needs not to worry? The reason Jesus gives is that the man who fell to robbers is more valuable than birds and flowers. If birds and flowers do not have to worry, then neither should the man who fell to robbers. So the man is valuable to God, but is God going to leave heaven and come down to help the man? No, God doesn't have to. God has a partner: the good Samaritan. A partner of God knows the value of the man who fell and will save him. That is why Jesus can say that no one will ever have to worry about clothes, food, friendship, forgiveness, or second chances. As long as God has partners no one will ever have to worry again. Being a neighbor means being cognizant of another's value. Valuables get immediate attention.

On the way to Jerusalem, Jesus stopped near Jericho to give sight to a blind beggar. That was a very nice thing for Jesus to do, but there is a problem. Jesus took away the man's sole source of income. He is no longer blind, so he has no reason to beg. Presumably, due to his blindness, he has no education, no job, no training, or skills. True, the man has his sight back, but what about tomorrow? What is he going to eat, and what is he going to wear? Should he be worried? No. As Jesus is about to enter the city, he sees a rich man in a sycamore tree. Jesus says to the man in the tree that He will have dinner with him. The man tells Jesus that he is going to give half his wealth to the poor. The man who was formerly blind does not have to worry about what he is going to eat or wear because Jesus has a partner who will take care of the poor. There is a very rich man in the city who is going to give half of his wealth to the poor. Jesus said, "Salvation has come to this house." Why did he say that? Jesus now has a partner. A true divine partner will recognize the value of a person in need.

Christ in the Gospel said do not worry about what we are going to wear or what we are going to eat. It is not because God is going to come down to feed us and clothe us. Rather, God has great partners. Never forget who you are and what you represent. When you wake up tomorrow morning, start the day by saying, "God, today you and I are going to do something great today, these are your hands, these are your feet, this is your mouth." You are God's partner. Never forget that.

Righteousness Means I Have a Relationship with God

Remember the parable of the lost sheep. So let's suppose I lost a sheep. I am not going to get it because I know what will happen if I do. I will return with the found sheep and discover that now two sheep are have wandered off in my absence. So I will go after the two, and while I am gone, five sheep slip away. I can't risk losing more than one sheep.

So I stand my ground, and I looked over my shoulder and see ninety-nine sheep looking at me. I said to them, "What do you all want"? They said, "We want you to go find him and bring him back." I replied to them, "I know what is going to happen if I run down that valley. You guys are all going to start to wander away." They assured me, "We are all going to stay here like a unified team. You will find us all here when you get back because we are behind you." And that is why Jesus called the ninety-nine sheep the ninety-nine righteous sheep.

Which leads me to say, that it is okay to be righteous. Yes, we all know that the repentant sinner always gets the party and the glory, but the righteous sheep become partners with God.

So let's turn to the elder son in the story of the prodigal son who is faithful to the father, every day he obeys all his commands. He comes home from work one day and hears music and a celebration for his long-lost brother. He is outraged. So this is my question: What is so wrong with the brother's anger? Isn't it normal to get a little upset, after all, the brother lost half the farm and the business, and now he is rewarded with a party? In order to understand what went wrong with the brother, we have to re-tell the parable with a positive twist. Let's see what the older son would look like if he were a righteous sheep. I will play the part of the son in my new version of the parable.

So there I am, the faithful older son, working in the field, and I look up and see my father. I give Dad a wave, and he acknowledges me with a nod. So I lean on my shovel and think, "Dad has not been the same since my younger brother left home. He never smiles any-more; he forgot how to laugh, he hardly eats because he lost his ap-petite, and he doesn't sleep well. He is a man in mourning. Often he just stands in the road and stairs into the horizon, hoping. I wish I could help him, but all I can do is just keep faithful to him." Anyway, after the sun goes down, I call it a day. I walk over to the house, and I hear singing and dancing. I ask the servant what the music is all about. He said, "Your brother has returned safe and sound, and your Dad slaughtered the fatted calf.' I said, "So he slaughtered the fatted calf I see. He must be hungry again. He must have his appetite back. And I bet he remembers how to laugh again. I am going to that party because I am going to enjoy seeing Dad smile again." This gladness is the example of a true partnership. The father was healed and the elder son was a big factor in my story. Bad things happen. Sons abandon their parents; sheep wander away from the fold. And yes, we are alerted to the problem with anger, but there are always solutions to problems. We are partners with God, when we manage our anger.

Not long ago my father went to the trout club, and his friend came over to him and said, "I brought my grandson to fish, but he hasn't caught anything all day. Can you help him out"? So Dad went to the pond and took a look at the grandson's fly-rod. He replaced the leader and put on one of his own "special" fly and gave the kid a suggestion on how to retrieve. Dad and the grandfather watched the child from the picture widow inside the clubhouse as he made three casts and caught three nice rainbow trout. Needless to say, the young angler was ecstatic. A few days later the grandfather bumped into me and told me the story. He said to me, "You know your father is a remarkable person." I said, "I know that." And then he said, "You are very lucky to have him as a father." And I replied, "I know that…that is why we are best friends." If only the elder son appreciated the character of his father, he too would be best friends with his Dad. Partnership means love has to triumph in the end. We must rid ourselves of jealousy, envy, and hatred. Only then will we be able to establish a strong partnership with the Father.

The Pharisees were upset with Jesus for eating with sinners and tax collectors, but righteous partners are never upset when the Lord is celebrating a victory. That is what is missing with the elder son in the story. Yes, the older son works hard, makes a great slave, a company worker, a business associate, but he is not very good at being a friend or a son.

Health Also Means Generosity: Don't Be Cheap

Remember the parable of the sower, how some seed fell on a path, some on rock, some in the thorn bush. It first appears to be wasting seed by carelessly scattering it broadcast. Had the sower been a little more careful, there would be no need to worry about rocks, paths, and thorns.

The total of the first Sunday collection when I came to St. Clement was 85 dollars. That is not a lot of money to run a church. A few weeks later I went to Home Depot to buy some grass seed. I reseeded the lawn which had a number of bare spots. Do you think a seed or two missed and landed on the sidewalk? At 25 dollars a bag, not a chance. Do you think I threw a few seeds to the birdies who were watching me? Are you kidding? Not at 25 dollars a bag. Did I put too much wrist action and a seed landed in the rose bush? Not happening at 25 dollars a bag. To me, it is the sower, not the rock or the path that is at fault. The reason why the sower in the parable can fling seed carelessly is that he has a bigger budget than I. The sower in the parable is carefree, generous; he is not worried or anxious in his sowing. Sure he risks losing some of the grass seed, but he ends up producing one hundred fold. I know of a wealthy parish that has a one hundred and fifty-thousand-dollar budget on the landscaping alone. They also have very beautiful grounds. They have no worries. I, on the other hand, have a reason to worry when the total collection is 86 dollars on my first weekend. The contrast between the sower in the parable and my sowing is striking: generous and superabundant versus stingy and miserly. If you are going to make great gains, you can never worry about your losses.

Returning to the good Samaritan, we see a man who had no limits to his generosity. The priest and the Levite had nothing to share. Fr. Jim Walther, my provincial, once summed up the parable of the Good Samaritan in this way: The thieves say "What is yours is mine." The priest and the Levite say "What is mine is mine." The Samaritan says, "What is mine is yours." If you want to make a difference, you have to be generous. Don't count your losses. Generosity is a sign of spiritual health and will need it if we are to be good partners.

If We Fear God, We Will Never Fear Anything Else

Fear is also an impediment to health, and there is a sure way of rooting it out of our lives. One day Isaiah the prophet had a vision when he was in the temple. He saw God seated on a giant throne. He reported that the temple was filled with the hem of God's garment. The hem of the garment is the stitching around the divine toe. That means the clothing around his foot filled the temple. It was Isaiah's way of describing the size of God. If the clothing that covered God's big toe filled the temple, it must mean that He is pretty big. By my estimations, that would make the throne He was sitting on approximately forty stories high, maybe fifty. That is the point of the vision. God is really big. If you or I saw God sitting on a fifty-foot throne, it would be safe to say that He would have our undistracted attention. It is a healthy, respectful fear. The reason it is healthy is that when we are afraid of God, it means that we will not fear anything else in life.

In the same vision, there are six Seraphs each with six wings. I always like to ask my students to give me a description of a Seraph. They always describe an angel. Actually, a Seraph is a snake. In ancient iconography of emperors, kings, and pharaohs, there are often cobras near the throne ready to strike. Seeing the snakes makes you think twice about harming the one sitting on the throne. You can think of the snakes as the bodyguards, the secret service, or guardian angels. What is disturbing about the vision of Isaiah is that the snakes are covering their heads and feet with their wings. Hardly the position they should maintain if they want to protect the king. That is because God is different from the other leaders who need protection. God who is big enough to occupy a throne that is higher than a fifty-story building does not need protection.

There is a great line in Psalm 23: "He sets the table before me in the sight of my foes." Picture yourself sitting at a picnic table with a nice juicy T-bone steak. A lion and a bear come out of the woods without warning and start walking over to your table. Apparently, they smell the aroma of the steak. What are you going to do? Are you going to leave the steak for the bear and the lion and run? Of course not. You will continue to sit there and cut a piece of the steak, put it on your fork, hold up the fork with the steak attached to it so the bear and lion can see it, and you are going to eat the piece of steak while they are watching. You will enjoy it too. You may want to tell the bear and lion how good your steak tastes: "Yum." Should you not be afraid? Not if you have a good shepherd at your side. If the lion and the bear get any ideas, they will get a bop on the head with the shepherd's staff. The point of the psalm is clear. If you know how big and powerful God is, you will never fear anything or anyone again.

There are two times in your life that you are totally alone: the moment just before you die and the moment you stand in front of a group of people to give a speech. Public speaking is one of the most high-stress jobs. We all have experienced a time when we had to address the crowd. Our heart races, and we start to feel a cold sweat. Why does this happen? We are good at talking. With animated passion, we discuss topics such as sports, politics, weather, and our feelings. We talk all the time. It doesn't make sense. Why would we be nervous about something we are good at and an activity we do all the time? That is because fear is in the head, it is not real.

The most fearsome task I ever had to do was my comprehensive exams. When I was accepted into the doctorate program, I knew I would have to face that dreaded requirement. When it came time to prepare for the exam, I knew how to make the fear go away. I wrote down every possible question that could be asked about the New Testament. I read many books which provided the answers to those questions. I wrote it down in a handy booklet. When the day finally came, I did not fear because I was basking in the light of knowledge. If you fear anything, turn on the light.

I was on vacation in Maine, and I went to the other side of the lake to catch the evening hatch. It was pitch dark when I left to return home. There were no street lights along the dirt road that meandered through a thickly wooded area that led back to the camp. I had my flashlight, but I wondered how dark it was if I turned it off. When I did, I could not see a thing. I wanted to know how far I could get without the assistance of the flashlight. I took a few steps forward, and I started to imagine that I was walking off the path into some tree branches. I didn't want tree limbs cutting up my face, so I held my hands in front of my upper body. Then I thought, "What if I walked off the road and into a ditch? I could break my leg and be left to die." To avoid that from happening, I decreased my speed and began to slide my feet forward, while my hands were held out in front of my face. Then I heard a twig snap. I immediately pictured a bear standing in front of me. I decided at that moment that I had enough of the darkness, and I reached for my flashlight. An amazing thing happened when I turned on the light. The bear that was in front of me disappeared, the giant hole and branches I was so worried about vanished as well. All the fear went away at the flip of a light switch. Fear is never real; it is in the mind. The only reality we should respect is the divine.

On the day of His resurrection, Jesus walked through the locked doors. I am sure the apostles were frightened because they thought they saw a ghost. They probably thought it was the angel of death coming to wipe them out for being such lousy apostles a few days before. Jesus had a small panic attack on his hands. So the first thing Jesus did was he showed them his hands. Why did he show them his hands? They didn't recognize his resurrected body, but they will recognize the hands. The hands are a really important detail of the story, and I think we should take a closer look.

When Jesus was walking on water during a storm, Peter jumped out of the boat. The other cowards stayed in the boat. The reason

Peter got out of the boat was he was not afraid of the water. Remember Peter is a fisherman. People who fish every day are not afraid of water.

Did you ever see a lake on a calm day? It looks like a dance floor—you could just run right across it. A stormy day is different. The heavy rain, water, and wind get so mixed together that you can't tell where the water ends and the air begins. The high winds generate waves. Peter gets out of the boat and starts walking on water, and he asked himself the question I would have asked: How do you walk on water with waves? Do you put your foot on top of the wave; do you jump over the wave? Do you walk parallel to the waves? I wouldn't know; I never walked on water during a storm. Neither did Peter. A wave crashes into Peter, and now he is knee deep. "Save me," Peter says. Immediately, the Lord extended his hand. At that moment something happened to Peter. For the first time, he was not watching others being saved by the Lord. This time it was personal. Just before he went under the waves, Jesus reached out his hand. Peter got a really good look at that hand because it saved his life.

Remember the blind man? Jesus spat on the ground and made the clay in his hands. The disciples gathered around to see what Jesus was doing. They got a really good look at those hands because they restored sight to the blind man. Before Jesus raised the dead girl, he took some of the disciples in the room with him. Everyone outside the room was laughing at Jesus because he told them that the little girl was asleep. Jesus took the dead girl by his hands. No doubt that those disciples were staring at those hands because they brought the dead girl back to life. If we want the fear to go away, all we have to do is recognize God's hand in our lives. If we can see the hand of God in our lives, we will no longer fear.

Everyone Seeks after Divine Privileges—Except God

If we can lower the stress, anxiety, and fear from our lives we will significantly contribute to our personal health. That is why the Bible addresses the issue of peace. Inner peace allows us to perform better, whether we are praying or working to make a difference for others. Sometimes health care can go to the extreme. We become so obsessed about our own existence that we forget the value of others. God is always about others. Let me illustrate.

If you were God, what are some of the perks you would enjoy? First, you would never die. No one could ever hurt you again. You would have total supremacy. Paul in his Letter to the Philippians says that Jesus did not grasp the perks that are enjoyed by the divine. He died so he could save, he suffered so that we would benefit from his graces, and he subordinated himself to obey and serve others.

Think about that. Which one of us does not want to die, who of us would like to be always right, make all the decisions, rule over others? Which one of us would not agree that it is easier to say we are sorry than obey? Which one of us wouldn't like to avoid suffering? Who of us would want to give up our hard-earned promotions, titles, or respect? Which one of us would not like to reach out and take the privileges that belong to the divine if we could? We don't want to die; we don't like to suffer, and we would like to be the one who is always right. These desires prove one thing. We are so unlike Christ. We need to be more like Christ. We fear losing our life, titles, appointments, privileges, respect, power, and money. If we were more like Christ, we would not fear these losses.

Terry Anderson was a journalist who was taken hostage for over seven years. When he was released, I learned that he lived nearby the parish. I asked if he would give a talk at the parish where I was working at the time. He arrived at the rectory an hour before the speech, so we invited him for coffee. While the church staff was speaking to him, the doorbell rang, and there were several journalists and photographers outside. They asked if they could see Mr. Anderson. I said, "Let me ask Terry." He told me to let in his colleagues and within a minute the dining room was filled with people. One of the nice things about having journalists in the room is that they know the right questions to ask. One of them pointedly asked Mr. Anderson what he thought was the most difficult part of his ordeal, and how did he get through it. He said when he was first captured, they blindfolded him and put him in a basement with no water to wash, no contact with the outside and family, and no sunlight. He didn't even know if he was going to live through the first night. "It was the darkest moment of his life," he said. "Yet, it was also the most powerful because it was at that moment that I felt closest to God."

How is that possible that one can feel close to God at the most difficult moments in life? If I invited the blind man from Jericho to give the talk at the parish, he would draw the same conclusion Mr. Anderson offered. Not only did Christ come to the blind man, but he had to go out of his way to meet and cure him. No one goes to Jerusalem by way of Jericho. There is a mountain pass full of robbers on the way. Apparently, Jesus took the longer route, put himself in danger, and risked the elements of a desert because there was some-one important for him to meet on the way: the blind man.

If I invited the Syro-phoenician woman to the parish to give the talk, she would tell us that "I was hundreds of miles from the Temple of the true God when my daughter was possessed by a demon. And yet, Christ came to me."

If I invited the thief on the cross at the time of Jesus' execution, he would tell us, "I was a thug, paying for my crime, nailed to a cross when Christ came to me and promised paradise." Christ comes to the out-of-the-way places and under the most unfavorable conditions.

That was the message Terry Anderson gave to us, "Never fear the darkest moment of your life. That is when God is closest." Therefore, never fear the darkness. Just tell yourself that you will be able to see the light much better when it comes.

Do Great Things Now, Because You Will Never Have This Moment Again

Once when I visited my mother in the nursing home, I asked her what she wanted to do. She said, "I want to get a pocketbook." Pocketbook? Okay, how hard can that be? It should be as easy as buying a wallet. You go to the section in the store that sells wallets, look for the cheapest one, grab it, take it the cash register and buy it. Well, we went to Kohl's. Did you know they have about a hundred pocketbooks of every shape and size? Mom was sitting in her wheelchair, and I was feeding her pocketbooks, one at a time. We took out the paper stuffing so we could examine all the inside features. I said, "So, which one do you want?" She said, "Can we go to another store?" We went to three. She finally picked one out at the third store. I noticed it was the most expensive. When we returned to the nursing home, my aunt Helen was there waiting. My mother was quick to show her the pocketbook, and they talked about it. They both looked at it for some time and then my aunt turned to me and said, "Peter, this is a very nice pocketbook." I said, "Yup." She said again, "Peter, I am not kidding this is a very nice pocketbook that you got your mother." I said, "I know because it cost enough." Then she said. "Oh, Peter, I was so close to my mother. If I could only have Ma back for five minutes, just five more minutes, I would mortgage the house and buy her the most beautiful necklace. Peter, you keep doing what you are doing, while you still have her."

I will never forget those words. Ten days later my mother died. Now I know why my mother wanted a pocketbook. She was going on a very special trip. Since her death, I have never forgotten my aunt's words: "If I could only have her back for just five more minutes." They are now my words. And now I am on a special mission to tell people not to put things off. Do it now. Be kind now, while you have your loved one. Be generous now. Live without regrets now. Heal your wounds, live without fear, and bind division. You may never have this moment again. It is necessary for us to have a healthy spirit. That is no fear, no anxiety, and little stress. With health, we can help others. We can be better partners of God.

Chapter Eight

Depend on God

The final skill we need to acquire is dependency on God. There is no better place to learn this than the desert. There is nothing in the desert: no food courts, no malls, no water, no shelter, no protection from the sun or enemies. It is there that you will need God again, and you will get close. You will depend on God for everything including the most basic needs such as bread and water. In the desert, you are forced to be a child again, and you will need your Father. You will develop and deepen a relationship with God.

The Best Work Is Never from Our Own Hands

The sand flea may be smaller than a fruit fly, but they have very sharp teeth. I was fly-fishing one summer evening, and the sand fleas came out to torment me. They had no mercy—they were all over me. I had two options: leave and miss out on the best fishing of the day, miss out on an exciting evening, miss out on a beautiful sunset, or stay and die. I remembered what my father used to tell my mother when he was fishing: "Just one more." So I decided to catch just one more fish. As I was about to leave, something happened. Out of nowhere, I felt this gentle breeze on my face. To a five foot eleven-inch guy, a breath of air is nothing. However, to a sand flea, it is a hurricane. And all the sand fleas blew away. To think, I was powerless against these aggressive biting insects. There was nothing I could do against them. A gentle breeze did something that I was not able to do. If I can be powerless against a sand flea, I can also be helpless against much more aggressive opponents in life. Sometimes we need help outside of ourselves.

Most Important Lesson in the Desert: Need God

Life for the Israelites was uncomplicated because God provided for their every need: food, water, and protection. Before they can become God's children, they have to learn to be dependent. Looking back at the Exodus experience, King Josiah recognized this particulate type of relationship to be hardest to maintain and the easiest to lose over time. And for a good reason. Maturity calls us to move from dependency to independence. In the desert, however, the Israelites did not have a choice. Self-sufficiency was not a viable option. When they left the desert and entered the Promised Land, they still had plenty of reasons to continue to trust God. For example, there was always the threat of foreign occupation, oppression, and droughts. The difference is that in the desert they had no options. In the Promised Land they did. They, instead, chose to look for means other than God because other resources were available. They became independent, and problems started to mount. Josiah had to return to what was lost. The answer to their problems was obvious when they read the book that chronicled the life in the desert. They needed to act like children of God again. They needed to need God.

The Way Life Ought to Be

Here is an exercise: picture Noah's ark in your mind. What do you see? Do you envision a large tugboat? Maybe one of the windows is half open, and two giraffes are sticking their necks outside. At another window, do you see a guy with a long white beard waving his hand as a dove flies by with an olive branch? Or instead, do you rather picture a large shoebox, about three stories high, a little wider than a football field and a little longer than a soccer field—no windows, just square walls with a hatch in the roof. If you envisioned the shoe box, then congratulations, you read your Bible. Scripture gives the dimensions and the shape of the ark.

What was it like in the ancient world to see the construction of this unusual structure? I can imagine the conversation between Noah and his neighbor. It would have sounded something like this:

Hey, Noah, that's a pretty impressive building. What is it?
It's an ark.
Ohhh, an ark…what's an ark?
It's a boat.
It looks like a shoe box, how are you supposed to steer the thing.
You can't.

It disturbed God that people were buying and selling, marrying, and re-marrying because they were living as if they didn't need divine assistance. When no one depended on God anymore, the divine voice reached Noah and said, "All right, everyone in the shoebox." Noah is now in the ark without oars, a sail, or a rudder, and there is a storm outside. He can't steer the boat which means he has no future, no direction, no control, and he is completely dependent on God—the way life ought to be. There is a reason why we call God our Father. We need Him.

It Is Okay to Need God Again

While I was enjoying my work as an associate pastor in New Jersey, my provincial asked me if I would go to Boston to make repairs on our church, rectory, and seminary facility. Bathrooms were not fully functional, the heating system (what heating system?), outdated wiring throughout, windows that would not open and close, and so forth. He strongly encouraged me to consider the move. The more I thought about it, the more I believed it was a bad idea. I heard all the terms and expectations. They did not come without their challenges. There was not much money to pay for the restoration, and repairs would not be cheap. The ambitious project had failure written all over it. I finally decided against the transfer. Before I went to my provincial to tell him "No," I thought I better get this decision right. So I called the holiest man that I knew at the time: a monk at Spencer Abbey. I asked him, "Can I see you for about five minutes?" We sat down, and I explained to him that my boss wanted me to go to Boston on a new assignment. I told him all the reasons I should not go. I expressed to him how much I loved my work in the parish (true) and how I learned to do the many tasks (Director of Religious Education, weddings) there really well. I explained how I started up a very successful youth ministry program that got kids off the streets. I even had five awards from the community to show for that effort.

After my defense, I asked this consecrated religious, "What do you think I should do?" He said this, "Peter, go to Boston." I could not believe he said that. Didn't he hear me? I asked him "Why?" He said, "Do you remember the first wedding you did? Did you know what you were doing? I said truthfully, "No." And the first time you had to say Mass at the prison. Did you know what you were going to say to inmates?" I said, "No." "Did you have any idea how to start up a youth program?" I said, "No." He said, "Go to Boston. Then you will need God again." It turned out to be the best advice I was ever offered. I transferred to Boston, and after three years the church and seminary were completely remodeled and restored. My dad, who supervised the project, said to me, "The work should have costs millions, yet you did it for just thousands." Dad recognized that there was some divine assistance on that job. Depending on God reflects a strong spiritual life because it represents a deepening relationship.

How to Repair a Damaged Relationship the Easy Way

That is why it is good to admit and confess our sins to God. It is the best reason to need God. We are weak. When I confess my sins, I make a list, so I do not forget anything. I picture that God also has a list of my sins. So while I am reading my sins, God is checking off his list. God says, "Okay, you got that one. Yes, another one. This next one is close enough, I guess." If that is how you picture the process, I ask you to reconsider your image. When you go to God and ask forgiveness, I want you to think of it as a "check-in" with God to make sure you have the most important matters in place: humility, honesty, and most of all, dependence on God. We are humble when we are admitting our sins. We are honest when we are acknowledging our missteps. We are giving God a very good reason why we need God. Our weakness is our proof.

Remember the parable of the Pharisee and the tax collector in Luke's Gospel. If you read that parable you will notice that the tax collector is justified by God because he is humble, honest, and needs God:

> But the tax collector, standing far off, would not even look up to heaven, but was beating his breast and saying, 'God, be merciful to me, a sinner!' I tell you, this man went down to his home justified rather than the other.

Pharisee or tax collector: Pick one. Let's see. On the one hand, the Pharisee will not steal from my grandmother by overtaxing her, will not sell my family into slavery because I do not have enough money to pay the levies, or have me arrested and incarcerated until I pay back the last penny. The tax collector, on the other hand, will. So just this once, I am picking the Pharisee. Fine, I understand that he is a little arrogant, but I can put up with a little egotism and conceit over cruelty and injustice. So naturally, when Jesus picks the tax collector I am befuddled. Here is the reason Jesus gave for choosing the tax collector. The tax collector presented a compelling case as to why he needed God; the Pharisee did not (Luke 18:9-14).

Recall the story of the prodigal son. The son takes the father's inheritance and spends it all until he is broke. Here is my question: What did the son buy with the money? Answer: He used the money on parties. How do I know this? The son had nothing left to show for his money. If he bought a house, he could sell it for food; if he bought a field, he could have grown some food or raised some cattle. He has nothing, which means he consumed the money.

Now that the son is at death's door, he is left with one option. He prepares a speech to convince his father to take him back as a slave. When the father sees him at a distance, he runs to him. While the son is delivering his prepared speech, the father interrupts the speech, cuts him off before he can ask to be a slave. Dad orders the servants to put sandals on his feet. Why sandals? Because slaves did not wear shoes, so the sandals provide dad an opportunity to make a status statement. Next, he tells the servants to put a ring on the son's finger. Why a ring? The ring represents family. Once his finger bears the band, he has been officially reinstated into the family. Lastly, the father slaughters the fatted calf. Why a fatted calf? So he can throw a party. Really? A party? Does he think the son needs another party so soon? Didn't the son have enough parties? Maybe some discipline would be in order here? If I were his dad, I would have said, "I am glad you had enough sense to come back, but go wash up and rest. And while you are resting I want you to stew over what you did to your poor father." I do not understand why the father throws him a party, which gives me an idea for renaming the parable: "Parenting: What Not to Do." Why did the father give his son so many nice things? The son gave dad a reason to help him.

I always wanted to fly fish. I love to watch the graceful casts. It fascinates me that one can catch a fish by imitating a tiny bug. So I started, and I never caught a fish. So I got books on How to Fly Fish for Dummies. Still no fish. Then I rented videos. Nothing. Then I took a fly tying class, thinking I would have flies that catch fish. I remember everyone in the class telling stories about all the fish they caught, how big they were, and what great fishermen they became. At the end of the course, I went up to my fly tying professor, and I said to him, "I do not have any stories about catching big fish like everyone else because I haven't caught a fish yet with a fly." He said to me, "I am retired, and I fly fish almost every day. Why don't you join me, and I will show you how." So I met him at a trout stream, and he directed me to cast out the fly and let it drift down the river. He said, "If you feel the fly graze against a leaf or scratching the surface of a rock, just lift up your fly rod, so the tip is facing the noon sun." So I let the fly drift, and I felt the fly tick on something at the bottom of the river, so I lifted up the rod, and I had a fish. I was so shocked that the professor laughed at my reaction: "Ha, ha, ha, do it again," he said. I repeated, and I caught another fish, he said, "Ha, ha, ha, do it again…" "And again." At the end of the day, I shook his hand and thanked him. I can usually articulate my thoughts fairly well, but the only words that came out of my mouth were: "That was great, like, you know, great." He said, "I had a lot of fun just watching you." True, he did laugh a lot. So why did he help me? Why did he share with me all the secrets that he learned from years of fishing? I gave him a reason. Here is the moral of the story. When you enroll in your fly tying class this winter, do not tell the professor how great you are and how many fish you catch. Give him a reason to help you catch fish. That is what the tax collector did when he went to the temple to meet God.

Hope: The Virtue for Those Who Depend on God

Paul, in one of his early letters, tells the Thessalonians to have "steadfast hope in our Lord Jesus Christ" (1 Thess 1:3). Later he says that hope is a distinctive Christian mark: "that you may not grieve as others do who have no hope." What is hope?

I walked into the community room during a Patriots football game, and my confrère was barking orders at the TV. He was offering such advice as: "Why are you running the ball. Let Brady throw the ball. You are making too many mistakes; the penalties are costing you yards. Move the chains if you want to win; three and out is not the path to victory; stop the blitz." All his suggestions were very good but ineffective because he was talking to a screen and not to those who have a direct connection to the decision makers of the game. Why was he expending so much energy by yelling at the TV? What good is sound advice without ears to hear? What exactly is he doing? I will tell you what he is doing. He is hoping. Hope means that the situation is completely out of your hands, and there is nothing else you can do but depend on someone else. We have all heard of the theological virtues: faith, hope, and charity. We like charity because we enjoy loving and get a sense of satisfaction when we are generous. We equally like faithfulness. One who is faithful to an idea, person, or community can make a big difference to others. We have to remember it is not always about what we do. Part of the spiritual success formula is to be completely dependent on God because sometimes things are completely out of our hands.

Faith and Love are Great, But You Need Hope to Complete Your Spiritual Life

One day I got a call at 2:00 a.m. from a hospital. The nurse said that there was a gentleman who wants a priest to anoint his wife who had just died. I said to the nurse that I thought she was already anointed. So the nurse checked the face-sheet, and it confirmed that the deceased was, in fact, anointed. The nurse told me I didn't have to come in. I could have gone back to sleep. However, before I hung up, I needed to know something. I asked the nurse, "Does the husband want me to come?" She told me, "He would like that very much." I said, "I will be there in a few moments." When I arrived, I walked into the room, took a look at the husband and said, "Mr. Lahaise?" I knew the grieving husband. He was the organ builder who restored our pipe organ in the church. When he saw me, he said, "Boy, am I glad to see you." I said, "Boy, am I glad I came." I love faith because it allows me to do great things and make good decisions.

Equally important is the virtue of love. Just before my intermediate Greek class began, the professor was chatting with us about his work as editor of the *New Testament Abstracts*. He said that he just read a 450-page book on the use and role of the word *hina*. *Hina* is a Greek term in the New Testament which means "in order that." Imagine writing a 450-page book on a word that just means "in order that." Naturally, the class gasped in horror at the thought of reading such a tome. The professor then said, "Oh, don't get me wrong. I wasn't complaining; I love my job." And that is why my professor, Dan Harrington, was one of the most respected scholars in New Testament studies: he loved what he did. Now if faith can get me out of bed at 2:00 in the morning, and love can elevate a person to be the most respected and sought-after of biblical scholars, then think what you can do with the combination of the two. We like faith and love because we can do something great with them both. We have something to show from these two virtues, but that is not the whole package. A successful life is achieved by all three virtues working in concert. We also need hope. We can do great things, but sometimes matters are completely and totally out of our hands. We simply need God.

Hope depends on God. It connects us to God and fosters a close relationship. That is why abiding success is in these three: faith, love, and hope.

Fulfillment: Good Luck Trying to Fill Bottomless Containers

We also need God in order to be happy. Happiness means fulfillment. If it is true that we are happy when we are complete, then we have a problem. We have these containers within us that we can't fill. Take my brain, for example. It is smaller than a football, but it is an infinite container. I can't seem to fill it with knowledge. A few years ago I got my licentiate to teach at St. John's Seminary. I got the degree because I need a licence to teach Catholic theology at a major seminary. After I got the diploma I told my family and friends, "This is it. I am done with school. This is as smart as I am going to get." Not long after I met the former director of my degree program to give him an article that I wanted to publish. He told me, "You should get your doctorate." I said, "Okay, I guess." So now I am back in school. Why? (I think it is a mid-life thing). The real reason is because I have a container I can't fill. I decided that I could be a better preacher, teacher, and writer if I spend more time with the experts in Scripture.

Suppose I was going to give you a crisp one-hundred-dollar bill. I bet you would not say to me after you take out your wallet: "I can't take it." Then I would ask: "Why not?" "Because it will not fit in my wallet; it is full. "Well put it in your bank account," I suggest. "I can't because my bank account is full."

Our heart is a container that can't be filled; a teenager's stomach can never be filled. Why so many unfillable containers? Does God want us to be frustrated, keep us from achieving happiness? I have answers to these questions.

I finished fishing and went back to the parking lot. There was a fisherman there putting on his waders. Naturally, he came over to ask me if I caught any fish. I told him I caught and released two nice fish. When I was done telling him what I used and where I was when I caught them, he felt the need to tell me about every fish he ever caught in his entire life. Then he told me about his work. I heard something about how important, great, insightful he was. Certainly, he left me with the impression that he is good at life. After a long while, he asked what I did for a living. I told him I was a priest, and I had a church in Boston. Before I could take a breath, he pulled out from his pocket, a pair of rosaries. I didn't see that coming. He explained. "I have a son with Down Syndrome who is the pride of my life. His life is fragile. I pray the rosary every day because I need God every day."

We have these bottomless containers but that does not mean we cannot fill them. I know this to be true from personal heartbreak. Six months after my mother died, I was in Bed Bath and Beyond to buy curtains for the guest room. Just when I found what I was looking for, a song came over the loud speaker that I recognized. It was one of those upbeat country songs, "forever and for always I will always be with you. I will never be separated from you." I remember hearing the song many times before at Kohl's department store when I took my mother shopping during her stay at the nursing home. The song brought me back to that store. It was as if I was behind the wheelchair, wheeling my mother around the aisles. I was fixed in these memories of being with Mom once again. I remembered her with such surprising clarity that I started to miss her all over again and then came the waterworks. Just at that moment when my eyes were filled with tears, at that precise instant of vulnerability, a woman who worked at Bed, Bath, and Beyond approached me and looked into my eyes, asking me: "Can I help you, sir?" I could have just leveled with her and said, "My mother passed away six months ago, and I heard this song, and it reminded me of her." She looked like a very nice girl, and she seemed like someone who would have said something like: "Oh that is so sweet" and she would have hugged me. I can also predict that the next day in the front page of the Boston Globe would read, "Priest Hugs Girl in BED, Bath and Beyond." I thought, "This would be not good." So I told her I was all set. As I was going back home, I thought to myself, "It has been six months, and I still miss her." When I returned, I went to the church. I said to the Lord as I pointed to my heart, "Do you see this. Do you see this?

It is empty, and you are the only one capable of filling it." I needed God.

Why did the prodigal son run back to his father? Because he had a container that he could not fill.

I believe that is why God gave us these bottomless containers that can never be filled. He didn't give them to us to frustrate us. He gave them to us so that He could fill them. It is okay to depend on God. It is okay to need God. That is how he made us, with infinite containers so we would never be able to fill them. He gave us a reason to seek the divine.

Live Like You Have a Fresh Start Every Day Because You Do

It is appropriate that we begin the New Year with a reading of the Book of Numbers. Numbers is the second to last book in the Pentateuch. The story begins with a census of all the names of anyone over 20 years old who were living in the desert after God delivered them from Egypt. After forty years, all the people on the census had died because of war, poisonous snakes, and desert conditions. The death of this generation is due to sin and disobedience to God. After forty years there is another census. Because everyone died, no one on the first census is on the new list except Joshua and Caleb. There is an amazing difference between the two censuses. The first census has the names of all those who died in the desert. In the second census, no one dies. Even during a battle with the Midianites, no Israelite soldier is killed. This is a new generation that will enjoy a promised land and no death in the desert. It is in this context that we are to understand the blessing of Aaron from Numbers:

The LORD bless you and keep you;

the LORD make his face to shine upon you, and be gra-
cious to you;

the LORD lift up his countenance upon you, and give
you peace.

So when Mary gives birth to Jesus, a new generation is born. Shepherds rejoice because it is a blessing. A blessing, according to Aaron, means no one dies because of sin. The two censuses in the Book of Numbers prepares us for what God does when he blesses. And God breaks sin and brings forth a new generation with the birth of a firstborn. With the Lord, there is a new start, a new beginning.

Who won the Super Bowl at the end of the 2012 season? The Baltimore Ravens. I only know that because I looked it up. Are Patriot fans still upset that Wes Welker dropped the ball on a three and long at the end of the fourth quarter during the AFC championship which allowed the Ravens to advance? No. Why? Because we are now in a new season.

Our church is a few blocks from Fenway Park. On opening day I noticed that all the Red Sox fans were cheery and jovial; they were proudly wearing their Red Sox memorabilia. I thought to myself, don't these people remember that just a few months ago the team suffered the greatest collapse in baseball history? Don't these fans remember that last year the Red Sox were in last place? Why are they so happy? Reason! It is opening day. It does not matter what happened in the rear view mirror because the players are looking ahead. It is a new start. Ironically, the Red Sox went on to win the World

Series after one of their most horrible seasons. The most quoted phrase that year in Boston was "Red Sox: worst to first."

That is why we can always have hope, always be happy, always be optimistic. There is always a new start with God.

I am a religious with a congregation that is called the Oblates of the Virgin Mary. The founder of our order, Fr. Pio Bruno Lanteri, had a motto, a catchphrase that helped many people: *Nunc Cœpi*. It is a Latin expression for "begin again." He would tell people, "Do not say that you are a loser. Don't say that you are the least in the kingdom. Say, 'Today I begin again.'" Live like you have a fresh start every day because you do. There is a reason to put our life with God. We always have a new day, a new beginning.

One of the most profound lessons of dependence on God comes from the Book of the Prophet Jonah. God asks Jonah to go to Ninevah and preach. Jonah does not want to go and for good reason. The Ninevites are the bad boys of the Ancient Near East. They are the worst kind of bullies who run around the Middle East and take everyone's lunch money. Jonah has a hunch that if he preaches to them and they convert, then God, who is slow to anger and rich in kindness will forgive them. Jonah wants the Ninevites punished, not forgiven. When Jonah gets there, he walks around the city for three days, and he preaches to them the worst homily I ever heard in my life. If I went to any church in the Archdiocese and gave the homily he offered to the Nivevites, I would be banished forever. Let's take a look at Jonah's awful sermon, "In forty days, Nineveh will be destroyed." In forty days? There is no mention of mercy, no mention of God, or contingent factors that could alter this bleak prediction. Yet, notice the small detail about the timing of the disaster: in forty days. Perhaps a hint of hope.

Still forty days has to be a procrastinator's dream. If I said to you, Christmas would be here in forty days, would you immediately stop what you are doing and start writing Christmas cards. Not a chance. If I told my students in my class that the paper is due in forty days, how many of them would be found in the library looking for resources that same day? Forty days is a long time. This is what is so amazing about the Ninevites. They put on ashes and declare a fast, immediately. The other detail worth noting is that every one of them participates in the fast and this includes children and the animals. Everyone. You can't find two people in the entire city to say, "I think this is very unnecessary, and I am not going to put ashes on me." The Ninevites put on ashes because it is a new day with God, a fresh start.

I am a Red Sox fan. I don't ask for much. I don't need to see the Red Sox win the World Series every year. I never insist that the Red Sox have the best pitching. All I want as a Red Sox fan is that the Yankees lose. That is not asking for very much. So a few years ago the Yankees were in the playoffs. I turned the radio on to catch the score. The Yankees were losing 5 to 0 late in the game. I thought it was safe to turn off the radio and go to sleep. The next morning, I woke up, and I decided to check out the results of the game. I discovered that the Yankees won 6 to 5. How did that happen? Character. They never quit. The Yankees never miss an opportunity. Someone on the team must have said, "We can beat these guys. We are stronger, and better prepared than anyone who puts on a major league uniform." Someone else on the team said, "Yes, victory is always more gratifying when you come from behind." This team was inspired, and they believed. That is why they win.

Character matters. Which means that partners believe that God can do the impossible: the greater the odds, the sweeter the ending.

Conclusion

We went to the desert to prepare ourselves to join God in his work. What did we discover there? Opportunity to develop skills that will make us better partners with God. These skills are not hard to acquire. Listening is easy because Christ is always right. Praying is delightful and inspirational: "Wow." Health means using God's gifts well. Depending on God gives us powerful leverage to take on any demand with success. We now have the tools to move forward. We are informed and enlightened from listening, filled with inspiration and conviction from prayer, charged with energy and good health, and empowered by depending on the divine. We can now become the best partners God could ever wish to have.

Part 3

Both

We have now arrived at partnership. We are well prepared from the skills of the desert. In part one, we looked at some of God's "skills." We are now ready to connect the two. What happens when the two come together? A story unfolds. It will have all of the components of a terrific story: sacrifice, boldness, commitment, and fellowship. This is what happened when I went to work for my father.

When my oldest brother turned sixteen, he went to work with my father for the first time. When he got home that afternoon, his t-shirt was soaked with his sweat, and he had smudges of tar on his face. I asked him, "What happened to you?" He said, "Roof job." That is what he said, but I knew what he was thinking, "I am not doing this for the rest of my life." He went to college, got a great job, sold his stock options and retired early.

When my younger brother turned sixteen, he went to work for my father. When he came home after the first day of work I asked him, "What happened to you?" He said, "Roof job." He went on to get a Doctorate in chemistry and he now owns a fancy cars and takes scientists to lunch.

When I turned sixteen, I went to work for my father. We both got up at 5:30 in the morning and put on heavy work shoes. At 7:00 a.m. we pulled a forty-foot ladder off the roof racks of the truck. At 7:15 a.m. we walk up the ladder each with an eighty-pound bundle of roof shingles. At 4:00 p.m. we fell asleep on recliners in the living room. I always wondered why Dad took naps after work. Now I know. And at 7:00 pm we caught striped bass in the Canal. When I went to work for Dad, he got a work partner. I got a new best friend.

Partnership is not about God barking out orders or us complying with divine whims. Allow me to return to the ballet analogy. When we are collaborating with God, there is grace and breathtaking beauty; simplicity and expression that cannot be put into words. A success story that is riveting and that embodies the best of emotion. When the Israelites completed their forty years in the desert, they were ready to show the world God and his significance. Now it is our turn to live the biblical narrative. We do not just read stories, we make the story. Before any dancer can hit the stage, they need to have balance, strength, quickness, and flexibility. Our version of these prerequisites is our ability to listen, communicate, stay spiritual healthy (elude anxiety, fear, scrupulosity, guilt, animosity, etc.), and depend on God. The desert experience gave us what we needed, and now we are prepared to advance with our collaboration with God. We are now ready for the majors. Partnership is a sublime and inspirational story. Our experience should yield (1) simplicity, (2) an abiding presence of God (Emmanuel), (3) service to others, and then (4) relax and let God finish the story. Our role is a son or daughter in this relationship. We have a father now and we about to receive our intellectual property as our inheritance. This means that we are given all the information, instruction, and guidance to be able to do the work of God.

Chapter Nine

Simplicity

Christ said I have come to give you joy that no one can take from you. In the Gospel, the merchant sold everything he had to buy the one pearl. Partnership means we are given what we need to reflect God in our life. That is the one pearl. We have just simplified our lives by becoming a child of God. We have the inheritance; we need nothing more. Allow me to illustrate simplicity. One time I angered someone. I forgot to mention the Mass intention. As I was getting a tongue lashing—"You bad priest"—I stood in silence with my head slightly tilted down. If you could open me up to look inside my soul at that moment, you would expect to see at that distressing instant a gathering of dark clouds of doom, which represented anger, disappointment, and bitterness. That is not what you would have seen. You would have witnessed happy sunshine and birds singing in my heart. How did I manage to keep my soul at peace, alacrity, and contentment? While I was enduring the verbal beat-down, I was thinking about my next fly-fishing trip. Simplicity means that we may not have everything, but we have one thing that really means something.

We need to always have our "one" thing that gives us peace. That is why God is always referring to himself as the "one" God, or as Jesus said, "That they may be one with me." The word "one" is a very important word in God's vocabulary. God wants us to consider him our one source of peace. It is there where we find simplicity.

Another Angle to Simplicity: Don't Forget to Look at the Big Picture Once in a While as You Manage the Particulars

Several years ago I went to Fenway Park to see a game. I noticed that there were a lot of distractions during the game. There was a guy in the bleachers yelling, "Let's do the wave." So we had a few rounds of jumping out of our seats throwing our arms in the air. Then people in my row had to get by me to use the restroom or grab a hot dog. Due to the fact that there is no leg room where I was seated, I had to stand up and suck in my gut so they could pass by me. Finally, everyone hunkered down, and they started to watch the game. It was at that moment that I heard a young boy crying behind me. Then I heard dad say, "What's the matter?" The young voice said, "My ball rolled under that man's seat, and I can't get it." I looked under my seat, and sure enough, there was a baseball. Naturally, I couldn't just reach under the seat and get it because my knees were jammed into the seat in front of me. So, I stood up and got down on my hands and knees. As I was reaching for the ball, everyone in the park jumped to their feet, and a celebration began. People were high-fiving one another, clapping, and cheering out loud. "What happened?" I thought. I got to my feet. Big Papi, David Ortiz, just hit a home run.

Let me ask you this question: Why do you go to Fenway Park to watch a baseball game? Do you go so you can sit in the most uncomfortable chairs you will ever sit in for four hours? I don't think so. Do you go so you can pay $7.50 for watered down cup of beer? I suppose not. Do you go to Fenway Park to see a Red Sox game so you can pay the highest prices for a box seat in any stadium in the country? I doubt it. You go to Fenway Park so you can see David Ortiz hit a home run…and I missed it. My experience at the ball game often reflects life. How many times are we so wrapped up in the many distractions, worries, and concerns of life that we lose focus on the things or people that matter most? We do not want to miss out on the most important things in life: our mission.

I used to have my own office. I had a picture on the wall of the *Madonna and Child*. Whenever I had an appointment or met with a couple, I would bring them to my office, and they always noticed the picture. Everyone was pleased and commented on the "nice picture." The reason why they noticed the picture so consistently was because it is the only thing I had in the room beside a few chairs. Once, one of my confrères came into the room and criticized me. "Your office is too bland; you need stuff." I asked, "What kind of stuff?" "You know, a few plants, some curtains. You need to hang a few pictures on the walls, and a throw rug would be nice." I said, "Then my office would look like your office." If I do that, however, then people would see all the stuff and suffer from stimuli overload. They will no longer notice the picture because their eyes had nowhere to focus. They would get lost in the mess. My visitors will no longer smile and say "What a nice picture." Too many things distract us in life as well. We get so much stuff in our lives that we no longer see the most important things or enjoy that which gives us peace.

Once, I went to visit a friend of mine. He asked me how I was doing. I told him truthfully that there was a strong rainstorm, and I discovered a leak in the roof. The basement flooded, and I had to bail out the boiler room. I had other problems I wanted to tell him.

I was just getting started, but he interrupted me. He said, "Oh, you have to go and see my new Zen garden. Just follow this path in the woods, and at the end, you will find it." That night we had dinner together, and he asked me "Did you see my Zen garden?" I said, "I went out to the end of the path, but I didn't see a garden. I saw a sand trap. The kind you find at the golf course, and it had a rock in it." "That is my Zen Garden." He said, "Let me explain. I have a regular garden with flowers and vegetables. When I go in my regular garden, I immediately notice the weeds, and I have to pull them up. Then I go back to my regular garden, and I see the green hoppers eating the flowers, so I have to spray the plants. Then I return to my regular garden, and my vegetables are gone because the animals are eating them at night. Now I have to build a taller fence. Every time I go in my regular garden, I turn into a man of war. I love my Zen garden because when I go there, I am a man of peace. The reason I have peace is because there is only one thing." Then he said, "Peter, do you get it?" When I first saw you today, you were upset about many things. You were a man at war. Don't forget who you are and what you are all about. Don't forget the one thing in life that gives you peace. You just focus on that one thing, and everything else is a ripple in the sand."

The day before my ordination I went to St. Catherine's Parish in Norwood to practice in preparation for the event. The pastor was there to spot me to make sure I was doing everything correctly. When I finished, he gave me some advice that I have not forgotten. He said, "When I was first made pastor I was full of energy, and I wanted to make a difference. I saw that the pews looked a bit tired and needed to be freshened up with a coat of varnish. To save the parish money, I bought a few gallons of spar varnish, I got some volunteers, and together we got the job done. Now, every professional knows that you cannot varnish over old shellac because it will not adhere properly. About a month later, everyone left church with varnish chips all over their clothes. It was a disaster. We had to hire professionals to sand the pews and re-varnish them. That same week, the sound system in the hall failed, and it happened during the middle of bingo. Naturally, that was my fault. Then the wedding couple wanted balloons in the church. I told them no. They are still mad at me. The church was no longer a source of joy, but problems." So he gave me this advice: "Peter, do not let the distractions take your eye off of what is really important." Don't forget why who you are and what you are all about.

It says in Scripture that the wise men from the east followed the star and "saw the child." What did they have to do to see the child? Let's do the math.

They dedicated a lifetime of study to become astronomers so they would understand the star when it appeared. They traveled far away from the east. They gave up their life-savings so they could give the child gifts that would be kingly and godly. That is a pretty hefty price to see the child. If the wise men were here today, they would tell us it was worth it. They recognized the one essential and dedicated their lives to it. That is simplicity.

The greatest archaeological discovery, ever, was the Dead Sea Scrolls because they give us information about the world at the time of Jesus. This discovery was not made by a scholar or an archaeologist. Two boys were throwing rocks in a cave in the Judean desert, and they heard something crash. They crawled inside the cave and found pottery jars with scrolls inside of them. They took pieces of the scrolls to antique dealers to trade them in for some candy money. The two boys were not the first to find the scrolls. There were other caves. Others went into the caves, saw the pottery jars, dumped the scrolls out on the ground, and took the jars. That is like throwing away the winning Megabucks ticket and keeping the empty envelope. It was the two kids that saw and recognized the treasure. Imagine all those years those scrolls sat there because no one except two boys could see that they were valuable. Remember what the pastor told me. That is why the light came into the world, so we can recognize what is important.

My friend Jack asked me to fish with him one very late afternoon just before the sun went down. I always like to fish with my friend because he knows all the best places. When I arrived, it was dark. He wanted to go to the yacht club where he is an associate member. Associate membership of a yacht club means a member who doesn't own a boat. Why would anyone want to join a yacht club that didn't own a boat? To access the boat docks. What is so important about the boat docks? At night the lights go on over the water. As you know, when you put the porch light on, lots of bugs draw near the light: mosquitoes, moths, June bugs, etc. The same thing happens when light is cast over the water at night. Clouds of shrimp and baitfish gather which of course means that big fish also draw near to feed. When we got to the docks at night, I never saw so many fish. We caught a lot of fish. At one point a yacht pulled up to the dock, and the guy got out and said, "We were at it all day and never got a fish." That is because all the fish in the ocean are right here under the docks. Who needs a boat to catch big fish? So what is my point?

That is what happens when you have isolated light; living things draw together in the light.

When we say, Christ is the Light of the World it doesn't mean that light fills the planet. It means that light is isolated in one location where all will gather to that light.

We have a daily Mass at 12:10 pm, Monday through Friday. There are usually twenty to thirty people in attendance. September 11, 2001, (9/11) was on a Tuesday. At the 12:10 pm we had 167 people. What happened? That was a dark day, and people gathered around to the isolated light.

Here is a question. How many Magi are in Matthew's Gospel? You probably recall the Christmas hymn "We Three Kings." Perhaps you got a card with a picture of three kings mounted on camels. If you think the answer is three, then you better read your Bible again. Matthew tells us there were three gifts, but he doesn't tell us the number of Magi. If they are carrying gold, frankincense, and myrrh—kingly and godly gifts—they better have an army of people to transport those riches halfway across the ancient world. If they only have three people, they are not going to make it.

Now picture this: King Herod is in his chamber, and he hears a knock on his door. "What is it?" "Magi from the East are here to see you." Herod then looks out the window and sees fifty, maybe a hundred kings, princes, astronomers, and the wise gathered from around the world at his door. That is what frightened Herod and the city of Jerusalem. Who is this kid that is drawing so many from all over the world? The child is the light of the world. He represents isolated light.

So, Keep It Simple!

Several years ago, I was asked to be on a committee. Our task was to prepare the agenda for a three-day meeting. So essentially it was a meeting about a meeting. The gathering of minds lasted for eight hours. The task at hand could have been accomplished a lot faster if we met at my father's conference room. Dad would have us stand around a set of blueprints covering a piece of plywood and two saw horses. I would hear: "Peter, get that wood on the second-floor deck, now." The meeting is over in less than a minute. However, this eight-hour gathering took place around a big table, and on it, plenty of snacks and beverages. Everyone sat down on very comfortable chairs, poured a cup of coffee, and we were there for the day. At one point someone asked what we should discuss at the three-day convention. I said, "We should talk about vocations, because, let's face it, gentlemen, not only are we replaceable, we will be replaced." After the meeting, my colleague, Tom Carzon, who was at the meeting, said, "You only said one thing all day." He was amazed that we were at it for eight intense hours, and I managed to speak only one time. He said, "But you know something? I remember what you said. In fact, what you said was the only thing I remember."

Yes, simplicity is vital for the spiritual life and a relationship with the divine.

It Doesn't Take Much to Achieve Greatness

Simplicity also means you do not need a lot to make a big impact. We often think that we have a lot in order to give a lot. If we have a lot, we can make a big impact in the world. But that is not how God works. We can make a big impact with very little. That is why in Scripture, God likes the crumbs that fall from the table because you can achieve a lot with so very little.

To illustrate this, let's go back to the first century. What would it be like to be a part of the crowd when Jesus multiplied the loaves and the fish? I picture myself sitting on the grass with a half a loaf of bread in my hand. I am so full from eating that I can't take another bite. Yes, I am one of the five thousand that was just satisfied from the loaves and the fish that the Lord blessed and multiplied. I am thinking that perhaps I can pocket this bread and have it for the journey home. If I don't eat it, I will keep it as a memento. I can pass it down to the next generation. The multiplication of the loaves will be one of the most talked about days in history. Think of what I could get on eBay for such an item. As I am holding the bread, one of the Apostles plucks it out of my hand and says, "Sorry, no doggy bags. The Lord wants all of the crumbs collected." Notice the exchange. I first took bread, and now I am giving back crumbs. This is the lesson of the multiplication of the loaves. It is not just about taking; it is about giving. We have to contribute as Christ contributed. The basket reminds me to put something in the basket after I have taken out. So here is the question: "Why does the Lord want the scraps? Jesus loves the crumbs because He can do so much with them.

Later Jesus told the parable of the rich man who ate lavishly. He later died and was tortured in flames. Why did the rich man go Gehenna? He did not attend to the needs of a poor man named Lazarus. What did the rich man need to do to help the poor man? Actually, not very much. He didn't have to re-mortgage his house, sell his yacht, trade in his stocks, or take a week off from work to help a poor man who came to his property for some food. According to the parable, all the poor man wanted from the rich man was a few crumbs that fell from his table. Such a request would not alter the rich man's life all that much. If the rich man were able to come back and to give us advice, he would tell us that it doesn't take much to get to heaven. One simply has to salvage the scraps because you can do a lot with crumbs.

Jesus loves the crumbs because you can do a lot with them. The Syro-phoenician woman, who is mentioned in Mark and Matthew, somehow knew that she would get on the Lord's good side if she mentioned "crumbs." After Jesus told her that it was not right to take the food of children and throw it to the dogs, she quipped: "I will take the crumbs." You do not have to give up everything to help others, but be sure to make good use of your scraps. I often ask myself: "What do I do with the crumbs that fall from my table?"

One late afternoon I decided to fish in Boston Harbor. I got out of the car, put on my waders, and walked to the water. There I stood for a moment, watching the sea in front of me, and I noticed a fish jumped, then another. There were hundreds of fish in front of me. I immediately called my friend Jack, who lived just up the street. Jack is an internationally known fly tier, and he would appreciate having such a phone call. Within a few moments, he was fishing with me. We were standing together. I was fighting a fish, and before I could land it, my line broke, and I lost the fish and my fly. I reached into my vest to get my fly box. Oh no! I just realized that I forgot to bring my fly box. No more flies. I stood there blankly looking out over the blue yonder while hundreds of fish were in front of me in a feeding frenzy. The famous fly tier asked, "What's the matter?" I said, "I just lost my last good fly." Jack came over to me and pulled out his fly box. When he opened it, a fly fell to the ground because the box was jammed with flies. Remember, he is a professional fly tier. I picked it off the ground, and he said, "Just keep it." I looked at the fly, and I could tell it was used. The feathers were all mangled, dry seaweed was stuck on it, and it looked like it had seen better days. I have to tell you, I had one of the best fishing days of my life. Now if you were to ask my fly-tying friend the question, "What did you do today that would be considered great?" I am sure he would never admit that he gave me a beaten-up fly that fell out of his box. He would tell you that he wrote another chapter in his book, that he tied flies for a special gift box for a valued customer, or that he paid the rent. If you rephrased the question, "What did you do with the 'crumbs' that fell from your table?" he would probably say, "I just made somebody's day." It doesn't take much to make a difference for someone. Jesus knows this, and that is why he collected the crumbs.

You Don't Always Have to Choose the Most Laborious Path— Seek Always the Easier Road to Success

Often we complicate life. We see the difficulties, and we recoil with dread. We get discouraged easily because our experience tells us nothing is easy, nothing is simple. Everything that has value comes with a high price, big demands, and long hours. This is not living in the moment of simplicity.

It was my day off, and I planned to go home and help mom with her spring garden. My plan of attack was to edge the garden, then prepare a bed with topsoil, lobster compost, and peat moss for the flowers. Then I would plant the annuals, water, and the job would be done in one day. I had a lot to do so I wanted to get an early start. So I charged into the house, "Okay, Mom let's go, go, go. You have to pick out the flowers at the nursery, and I will get the bedding material." She said to me, "Can we go to Mahoney's?" I said, "That is down the Cape." She said, "They have nice flowers there." I must have driven past one hundred nurseries before we drove over the Cape Cod Canal Bridge. Naturally, we had to have lunch at the Clam Shack in front of the entrance of Falmouth Harbor where you can see all the boats coming and going. After lunch, she wanted to stop to get homemade ice cream at a place called "Sundae School." You can't go down the Cape without taking in the beach. We finally got to the nursery. We split up. She went to get the flowers, and I went to the "Bed, Bath, and Beyond" section of the super-nursery to get the topsoil and peat moss for the bedding. We were going to meet at the cashier. When I was done, I waited patiently. After some time, I saw her approach. I said, "That is it, only one plant?" She had a small bush with thistles and a few small yellow flowers. It was the oddest thing they had in the place. I thought, "We came all the way down here for this?" When we got home, I asked her where she wanted me to plant it. She said, "Next to the front door so everyone will see it." I dug a big hole and made a nice bed and planted the one plant that we bought. After dinner, I went home. During the drive, I had time to reflect on what had just happened. I didn't get a lot done—not what I planned—but we had fun.

Two months after my mother died, it was early July. Dad and I were walking into the house, and right at the front door entrance was this large bush completely covered with little yellow flowers basking in the glory of the noonday sun. Dad said, "I love that bush." I said, "So do I."

Of course, my mother knew that the annuals I wanted to plant would have been gone and forgotten a long time ago. She knew this plant would be a fireball of beauty every year. She also knew that when I looked at it, I would not just be seeing a magnificent plant, but I would also never forget the terrific day we had together when we got the plant. I think my mother knew something about the way God works with us.

Don't Let the Little Things Escape Your Notice

Simplicity also means that you are going to find opportunity. Remember, you are working with a divine partner so be on the lookout for opportunity. I was on vacation when I drove up to a lake. When I put the truck in park, a green inchworm dropped on the windshield right in front of me. I turned to my brother and asked him, "David, do you have any of those green worm flies." He said he had a bunch of them. I said, "Can you give me a few of them." My father and brother took off to the middle of the lake. I stayed at the edge where the trees where hanging over the water. Just as I thought. A strong gust of wind rocked the branches, and immediately green inch worms fell into the water and were gobbled up by the fish. So I took out my green worm fly and cast it under the tree. As soon as the fly hit the water, I had a fish. I knew I was going to have a really good day. When the green worm dropped in front of me while I was still in the truck, I consumed valuable information. I like to think God gave me insight. When I fish with Dad and my brother, we usually venture off to different locations until someone figures out how to catch the fish. We are a team. On this particular day, they didn't catch any fish in the middle of the pond because they were all under the trees near the shoreline. I shared my findings, David provided the green worm flies, and Dad bought lunch. We all had a great day. God wants to give us information, but we need to pay attention to simple signs.

Simplicity Breeds Gratitude

The reason why simplicity is essential for your partnership is that achievement is no longer laborious, hard, or unpleasant. Joy is the typical emotion that comes from working with God. If the job is done right, you should feel gratitude, not exhaustion or stress.

Every letter by Paul (except one) begins with gratitude to God. In 1 Corinthians Paul appears to be happy for the gifts that God will bestow on his Corinthian Church. But just after the thank you to God, the fireworks begin. Paul seems to have nothing good to say about them. Paul chastises on many levels. They are disloyal to one another. They are divided. Paul has to reprimand them for taking the Eucharist unworthily. Paul is horrified that someone in the community is sleeping with his mother-in-law. Christians are taking other Christians to court and suing one another. Some are using their spiritual gifts for their own aggrandizement, while at the same time shaming and putting others down as if they are less gifted. So why does Paul thank God before he chastises?

Paul is not grateful to God for the past, but for the future. He sees that despite all of the present atrocities, God encourages future growth and maturity. For Paul, it is okay to anticipate graces in the future. We always look to the past to find reasons to thank God, and this is noble. But Paul is always looking to the future. If you are continuously looking at the past, you are facing the future with your rear end. Paul always faces the future when he walks forward. Things may not be impressive now, but with Christ, things will be great in the future. So he faces the future with hope and gratitude.

Yes, I look to the future when I thank God. I thank God because I hope soon to see the ordination of the seminarians I teach. I am grateful that I will see my brother and his wife this coming Thanksgiving. I am grateful that I will enjoy the resurrection to new life. It is okay to anticipate that God will always be there for me in my future, and because of that certitude, I can be grateful.

Many people look to the past and have nothing for which to be thankful. Those in prison, or on death-row may look to the past and probably do not feel a lot of gratitude. An unsung hero in a nursing home, who has to stay in bed all day because someone decided not to come to work, does not feel a lot of gratitude. Those who lost their home, their job, their family or soulmate do not feel a lot of gratitude for the past. You, who are reading this book may not feel gratitude for what has happened to you in the past. Paul in this letter tells those who have nothing in the past to make them grateful, that they are looking in the wrong direction. They need to turn 180 degrees and look to the future. It is the path forward that will lead to hope, grace, and bliss, not the past.

There is a legend about a guy who was returning home from work. He saw a stranger who was looking at something in his hand. The man went over to see what he was looking at. He had an enormous diamond in his hand. The man said to the stranger "That is the biggest diamond I ever saw. It is breathtaking in its beauty. Where did you get it"? The stranger said, "I found it during my travels. Since you like it, why don't you take it? The man was overcome by the stranger's generosity. He wrapped the diamond in his handkerchief and placed it in his backpack. When he got home, he pulled down all the shades and put the diamond under his lamp. He admired the dancing light. He then took a velvet cloth and wrapped it up. He put it in the safe. He could not sleep all night. The next morning, he went into the safe and took out the diamond and searched for the stranger. When he found him, he gave him back the diamond and said, "Sir, here is your diamond. I would rather have the thing you have in your possession that made it so easy for you to give up this diamond." Note that the man recognized that the stranger had something in his possession that was far greater than a priceless diamond.

I share that story with you because we are that stranger. We are the one who has possession of a great treasure. That is what Paul is saying in the opening of his First Letter to the Corinthians. We have something that is so great that it will be easy for us to give up our other treasures. Here is the lesson. We have something very great. We just need to recognize it. We need to be convinced that working with God will put us in touch with great opportunity. We need to see it.

Salt Is Cheap but Indispensable

One place we will always find opportunity is with our neighbor. We are familiar with the rule. Love God; love neighbor. Let me show you how I found opportunity in this commandment. I added church bells to the outside of the church. I thought it would be nice to give the neighborhood a monastic feel in the middle of the city while offering the locals a sense of the presence of God. I was pretty happy with my little contribution. I got a phone message from one of the neighbors. It was a colorful message with words that are not fit for publication. Apparently, he works at night and sleeps in the day. I shut down the bells and have not played them since. Why should I honor his request? He was rather rude and hurtful with his message. Answer: "Love Neighbor." Because he is my neighbor he gets preferential treatment, regardless if he likes me or not. Think about what the world would be like if everyone lived the "Love Neighbor" principle. That is why Christ calls Christians the salt of the earth.

During the sermon on the mount, Jesus told his hearers that they were the salt of the earth. What exactly does this mean? I will give you a hint. It has to do with simplicity. One night I walked into the TV room, and some of the guys were watching a cooking competition on the Food Network. There was a chief that visibly wanted to win. He was running from one end of the kitchen to the other grabbing ingredients, mixing, and chopping. He had food cooking inside the oven and four skillets were going at the same time on the stove top. He was throwing all kinds of stuff in the blender for his sauce. He plated, and his steak had perfect grill marks that rested on top of creamy mashed potatoes with a rich looking sauce. Surely, this guy is going to win. He lost. He forgot to put salt on the food. The judges asked him. "Did you forget the seasoning?" He put his head down and said, "Yes."

He forget to use salt? Are you kidding? Salt is the cheapest thing in the kitchen. It is the easiest thing to do. You just shake it on the food. It does not require exact temperatures or measuring spoons. When Christ said that we are the salt of the earth, it is a little insulting, don't you think? Can't I be a lobster tail or the *à la mode* to the meal, or perhaps a hot chili pepper? Salt is the least expensive item in the kitchen, and it takes only a little skill to use well. Yet, without it, everything is bland. What we do as Christians does not cost us very much, and what we do is not difficult, but without living Christ's life (i.e., love neighbor), the world is tedious, dreary, and void of meaning.

Here is a good example of what it is like to be the salt of the earth. One time I had to go to one of those all-day workshops. I told my mother that I would not be able to see her that day. At the time, she was in a nursing home so she really looked forward to having visits. When it was noon time, the hosts told us that there was a two-hour break for lunch. I thought I would have enough time to visit Mom after all. I stopped on the way to get her an ice cream shake before I got to the nursing home. When I arrived, Mom was alone in her room sitting in her wheelchair slouched over fast asleep. I tapped her on the shoulders, and she looked up and saw me standing over her with a goofy smile holding her mocha shake. She was so surprised to see me. She said, "I thought you had a workshop today." I said, "I did, but I am on a long break." She was so happy and surprised to see me that tears welled up in her eyes. I said, "Mom, it's just me," She said, "You told me you couldn't come today, but I was still hoping." That is salt. What we do as Christians does not cost us much, and it is easy to do, but without us, the world is dull. No, we are just salt, but remember this: we are the best thing that ever happened to the world. And you need to believe this. Here is the litmus test if you are salt. When we are salt, people will say about us: "Boy am I glad I ran into her, I am glad I ran into him."

I am grateful to a lot of people who were really good at being the salt in my life. One time Dad said, "Let's go fishing." I said, "It is January, the middle of winter. What are we waiting for?" So we went to the Salmon River. Predictably, when we arrived, we were met with a severe snowstorm. Of course, it was blowing sideways. I was wearing so many layers of clothing that I looked like the Michelin tire man. For obvious reasons, we were the only ones on the river that day. We pulled up to a parking lot and walked to the riverbank where my father said he caught some fish a few years earlier. We fished all morning—nothing, not even a nibble. We were about to make the last cast and call it quits when in the distance we saw someone walking toward us. When he reached us, he asked, "Any luck?" We said, "No, not a hit." He said, "Funny, I've fished this pool the last few days, and I didn't do anything either. I think the fish left this location and headed up to the next pool. Now, if you go past the bend in the river, just beyond the rapids there is a deep hole. You should do well there. He told us what to use. After he wished us luck, he left. I said to my father, "I know we are crazy for being here in this weather, but what is he doing here?" He said, "He is a guide. He has to be here so he knows where the fish are and what they are feeding so he can put his clients into fish." I said, "If he gave us free advice, we better take it." We went to the hole and fished all day. We even skipped lunch and stayed until dark. That night we found a restaurant, ordered some food, and raised our glasses. Dad said, "Here is to a great day of fishing." I said, "Boy am I glad we bumped into that guy. To think we were just about ready to call it a day and he turned us from quitting to staying." When I think about it, the guy just told us where the fish were. And yet he made such a big difference to us. That is what it is to be the salt of the earth. If we are true salt, people will say the same about us, "Boy, am I glad that person came into my life." Simplicity means there is opportunity for us to be a source of greatness for others. And simplicity also means that it does not take much to make a difference. That is why our divine partner loved the crumbs that fall from the table.

Chapter Ten

Be with Him

Once you begin to work with God you will discover that your most important job is to be with Him. Talk about simplicity. Good fathers like to be with the kids. If only the kids what to be with the father. That has to be our desire. Mark reports something about what Jesus said that no other Gospel writer mentions.

> He went up the mountain and called to him those whom he wanted, and they came to him. And he appointed twelve, whom he also named apostles, to **be with him** (Mark 3:14).

This is a very profound statement because Mark tells us why he chose the twelve; "to be with him." My dentist gave me a lecture on my last visit. Not about my teeth. They are in great shape. He discussed my diet: go veggie he told me. No meat, he claimed, is better than less meat. He gave me compelling statistics, showed me websites, and he even quoted the Bible. He said that if I could avoid heart disease, I could live to be hundred years old. I said, "Why would I want to live to be a hundred years old?" Anyway, he gave me something to think about. Later that same day I went home to see Dad, and he said, "Peter, I feel like having a nice steak, what do you say?" I said, "Funny you should ask me that, Dad, I was thinking about that all day today." I enjoyed my steak that night because I was eating it in the company my father who was enjoying not only a great steak but great health at the age of 85. What if I didn't have dinner with Dad? Instead, let's say I was having dinner with my dentist that same night. I would not have ordered steak because I know I would not enjoy it. If I did order steak, I would have felt very uncomfortable. In fact, I probably would have gotten another lecture. Or perhaps dining with my dentist may have inspired the beginning of a new practice. My point is this. We make our decisions in life by the company we keep. There is an advantage when we are with Christ because such a relationship helps us with our attitudes and decisions in life.

"Being with him" confirms our relationship. When my mother died, I was heartbroken. After I made a few phone calls, I needed some time to be alone. I went to my room and sat on the corner of the bed, and I pictured her with the Lord. Jesus told her: "You can go back if you want." My mother looked up at the glorious beatific vision, then she looked over the Lord's left shoulder and saw the seven choirs of angels singing. She took a look at her new room in the divine mansion, and then she saw her mother. They were best friends. And after seeing all of that she gave her answer: "I am not going anywhere, I am staying right here." Then Jesus said to her, "What about your family?" My mother said, "They will be fine; they know that I am with you, and if they don't know, my son is a priest, and he will tell them."

It Is All About Who You Know

Here is another incentive for you to desire to be with Christ. I organized a small gaggle of chaperones and thirty teenagers to go to

Denver to see Pope John Paul II on the occasion of World Youth Day. Thousands of us were gathered in some field waiting when suddenly five helicopters appeared on the scene. First, the bishops processed out on the stage then the cardinal. When the Pope stepped out, there was a thunderous reception from the people. I looked over the shoulders of thousands in front of me, and I saw a white dot. A few weeks after I got back from Denver my pastor went to Rome for vacation. When he came back, I asked him how it went. He said, "It was fabulous." He said, "I got to concelebrate Mass with the Holy Father in his private chapel." I said, "No, I don't believe you. Only famous people can get close to the Pope. Then he took out several 8 ½ by 11 photos of him with the Pope. I said, "What? I took thirty-two people to see the pope, to evangelize our youth, and all I got was a white dot. You go to Rome on vacation, and you get glossies. That is not fair." He said, "What can I say; I have connections." Then he said, "Peter, it is all about who you know." If that is true, then there are advantages when you are with Christ.

I came to St. Clement Shrine in Boston to initiate a restoration of the church and seminary. We took out a half a million-dollar loan. The first thing we did with the money was we hired an architect to assess the needs of the building. He finished the feasibility study and concluded that we would need at least 10 million dollars to do the major bulk of the work. I was devastated. I thought, "How am I going to do this? I am a priest; I say Mass and anoint the sick. What am I going to do? Finally, I thought, I can't do this job, but I know someone who can. I know a professional contractor who I could trust. So I met him at a restaurant, and I said, "Dad, your hired." We got the job done, and it didn't cost 10 million. Sometimes we think we have to solve all the problems. Sometimes we try to shoulder all the burden. But we will be far more successful if we just know the right person.

Jesus tells the man born blind: "Go to the pool of Siloam and wash." So he goes to the bottom of the hill, lowers his hands in the water and splashes his eyes over and over again. Then he steps away from the pool rubbing his eyes. He takes his hands away and looks up for the first time in his life his sight is filled up with light, color, depth, and height. That moment will forever be etched in his mind. After the event, everyone begins to ask him, who opened your eyes? Why does everyone need to know who opened his eyes? Because it is about who you know. Jesus came so that we would know him. Whenever we encounter a mission impossible or a difficulty in life that we cannot handle, remember, it is not about us. It is really about who we know.

How to Be in a Perpetual State of Happiness Without a Penny in Your Possession

It was snowing all weekend, so I was on foot to the hospital for a few calls. I walked back to the church, and I decided to enter through the back door. When I got to the driveway, I saw a homeless gentleman looking for cans in the recycling bin. I knew him. He was a regular. I was happy that he helped himself to the cans. So I called out to him, "How's it going?" He stood up straight and took two steps toward me. As he was walking, an avalanche of snow slid off the church roof and landed where he had been standing precisely at the recycling bins. He looked back and saw the pile of heavy wet snow and said, "God sent you to save my life." He reached his hand into his pocket, took out a one-dollar bill, and handed it to me. That is what he did. Let me tell you what he did not do. He didn't take out a wad of money, thumb through the twenties and the tens until he came to a one-dollar bill, pull out the one dollar and hand it to me, as so many of the faithful do on Sunday before the collection basket passes by them. Nope. He went into his pocket and took out his only dollar. I said to him, "I am not taking this." He said, "It's not for you; it is for God. He just saved my life." Then, he walked away humming cheerfully.

I stood there for a moment reflecting on what just happened. If you are homeless, and you have to look for cans in recycling bins during a storm to get a few nickels together to buy a coffee or some hot soup, then you are probably not having a very good day. And yet, he was the happiest person I saw all day because he knew that someone was watching out for him, someone cared about him, someone loved him. Christ came so that we could be with Him.

Love Is Not About How Much You Give, It Is About What You Have Left After You Give

"Being with" typically means a relationship that is based on love. I walked into a Sears. The reason I was there was that the store had something I wanted, and I had something the owners of the store wanted. The salesman came over to me and said, "Can I help you?" When I told him I wanted a snow blower and not a pair of men's socks, he got excited. He said, "This is a great time to get a snow blower because our best model just went on sale. Not only is the price reduced, but it has a five-year warranty. We will come to your house to fix it if it needs repairs or parts. And not only that, it is easy to use. It comes with an automatic start switch, so you do not have to pull a cord." I said, "I'll buy it." We walked together to the check-out. He said a few funny things about buying a snow blower at the end of the snow season, and I laughed, and I said a few funny things about trying to purchase a snow blower at Home Depot, and he laughed. In the end, we shook hands. I even got a pat on the back just as I turned to leave. Yes, I liked this guy because he gave me a good price, a warrantee, and a good snow blower. He liked me because I was an easy sell. He was a nice guy and all, but I do not call that love, I call it shopping.

Whenever I do something nice for someone, and they return the favor, God does not call that love; he calls it shopping. So Christ came to clarify what love actually means. It happened not long before he died on the cross. Standing near the treasury, he observed a poor widow donating two copper coins. It was everything she had. It was at that moment that Jesus redefined love. Love is not about how much you give, (you can get it back). It is about how much you have left in your wallet after the giving. Christ gave up his life on the cross which resembled the same principal as the widow: God the Father gave everything he had: his Son. The Son gave everything he had: his life. When Christ said, "Love one another as I have loved you." He is inviting us to join him. Do not hold back.

What Do You Have Left After You Give

I used to rake leaves after school. I was saving the money for something big. The plan was to go to the mall Saturday afternoon after Mass and buy stuff. When it was time for the collection, I took out my roll of money from my pocket, and I flipped through the fives and tens until I found a one-dollar bill, the usual standard for church collections. I pulled it out and put the rest back in my pocket. As the usher came closer, I had a thought, "Put it all in. Go ahead. Do something great once in your life. Nothing says I love you more than cold hard cash. Show God how much you are willing to give." I sat there cold as a stone and unmoved. Just as the usher moved the basket in front of me, I dug into my pocket and dropped the whole wad. When the usher took one look at that money, he pulled the basket away from me as fast as he could in case I changed my mind. And then in a flash, it was gone. But my relationship with God forever changed that day.

Generosity is the superglue to a relationship, but if you want to dissolve a partnership, just do the opposite: be cheap. While I was on vacation, my brother suggested that we make a stop at the "Sundae School" ice cream parlor. I got in line, and the guy said, "What'll you have? I said, "A small vanilla." I ordered a small because most of these ice cream shops take a small cup and they pile it on until they turn a small into an extra-large. He got the scoop and reached into the bucket and put a scoop of vanilla in a small cup. I figured he was going to reach down and grab another scoop. Instead, he put the cup with the ice cream on a scale. Apparently, he had put too much ice cream in the cup, because he took some of the ice cream from the cup and put it back in the bin. As I watched him do this, I thought to myself, "What a cheapo." While this was taking place, I noticed directly in front of me was a large glass container with the word TIPS. I have to say he didn't inspire me to dig deep in my wallet and fill his jar.

That tip jar, however, did make me think. Picture this: all of us have a large tip can before God (some of us have a tip barrel), because we are always asking God for favors. We have a lot of needs. If we want God to fill up the tip jar, then we better inspire him by piling on the good works. We may think that we are ordinary and "small" like the ice cream cup, but we can still pack it in. Generosity seals relationships

A Relationship Should Always Mean "Welcome to the Family"

The gospel is calling us to be real, that is, someone who genuinely loves others and God for all the right reasons. That is how you establish good relations with others. You have to be authentic. Paul wrote a powerful letter on a relationship between a slave and his owner.

It is astonishing that one of the most important human achievements in history was done in a Roman prison. Paul wrote a letter, and we are still reading it two thousand years later. Paul's base camp was Ephesus. If you happen to be standing on the shore line at Ephesus and look directly across the sea, you will be staring in the direction of Corinth. If you turn around exactly in the opposite direction and travel eighty miles as the crow flies, you will come to the Lycus Valley. There are three cities nestled together. In one of those cities there lived a rich man who owned one of the first Christian Churches. They did not call it St. Peter's or St. Clement. They probably called it the rich guy's living room.

This wealthy man had a slave who committed the ultimate no-no. He ran away. It would make sense if he ran to Ephesus. It was there that he probably met Paul and was converted. When Paul was in prison, the runaway slave helped him. Why did Paul need help while he was in prison? Roman prisons only offer a cell. They do not provide food, healthcare, or internet access. You need contact with the outside to stay alive. While Paul was in prison, he sent the slave back to his owner. Why would Paul say goodbye to the guy who was helping him stay alive, to return so he can mop the rich guy's floors and clean toilets? Paul wrote a letter telling us why. To fully appreciate what he wrote, let me tell you what I would have written if I was in that same prison.

Dear Philemon,

I am in a Roman prison. It is filthy and overcrowded. I fear I am going to get very sick and die if I stay here any longer. Here are the facts. I did not kill anyone; I did not steal, and I paid my taxes. The only thing I did wrong is "love God." For such a small offense, all I need is a little money to bribe the judge. That is how things are done here. I hope you can help me so I can get back to my full-time job of bringing Christ to the world. Thank you.

Sincerely,

Peter Grover

This is what I would have written. This is what anyone might have written. This is not what Paul wrote, and that is why we are still reading his letter in church two thousand years later. He tells Philemon to receive his former slave as a brother. Tell him when he arrives, "Welcome to the family." In other words, Paul was telling the rich man, "If you don't take this guy who committed the ultimate crime in the Roman culture, if you do not take this slave who deserves death or a severe punishment, and if you do not greet him with enthusiasm, with an embrace, and give him a nice ring on his finger, fresh clothes, a place of honor at your table, and treat him like your favorite brother then you are missing out on living the most fulfilled life you could live. The rich man can have a brother if he accepts his slave as one. Let me illustrate what Paul is offering.

Our parish was in the rotation to go to the homeless shelter once a month to provide the dinner. Our specialty was Shepherd's Pie. The whole meal was in one long pan, so portability and cleanup were great. There was a long table at the shelter, and we set the table and put out the food. We had the main course, salad, bread, dessert, cans of soda, and water bottles on the table. We stood behind the table, and the hungry men would grab a paper plate, and we would dish out the food on it as they walked along the other side of the table. They would take some bread and a soft drink, have a seat and eat their meal. We stayed there for a little over an hour serving the food, and then we packed up to go home. I remember the ride home. I always had a good feeling inside that I was able to give something back to those who didn't have. I always enjoyed the feeling of generosity. Then…

I was greeting the people after Mass one Sunday just before Christmas. A gentleman handed me a wad of money and told me to use it to help the poor. After some thought, I decided to give it the Little Brothers of St. Francis because they worked with the homeless on the street. That is, they were in hand to hand combat with poverty all day. Two weeks later they sent me a thank you card. On the front of the card was a picture entitled "The Little Brother's Thanksgiving Meal." There was a large table all set with lots of food on it. The Little Brothers were seated around the table and between each of the brothers was a homeless person. They had their arms locked around each other's shoulders. I couldn't take my eyes off the picture. I was studying their faces. One of the homeless men looked so happy; he was laughing out loud. The second homeless man was in a presidential pose with his head erect as if he was the most important man in the world because he was invited to dine with holy men. The third homeless man in the picture had his eyes on the food as if he hadn't eaten in days. There was a difference between the brothers of St. Francis and me. I served food to homeless people, but the ones in the picture were not homeless – not that day. Today they were part of the family. Partnership with Christ always means the family will get bigger and closer. When we are with Christ we get to live the most fulfilled life, as Paul said in his letter to Philemon. When we are with Christ, we are family, which makes us brothers and sisters. So being with Christ means we are in a family. We are constantly seeing the family grow when we turn people into brothers and sisters. Here is an example.

One of the disadvantages to having a birthday on September 6, as I do, is that I always received birthday presents that related to school: notebooks, pencil boxes, and school clothes. My brother, on the other hand, who has a birthday in January, always got sleds, ice skates, and fishing tackle. One birthday I got a bike. It was special because I became the first kid in the neighborhood to own one with three gears. I took it out for a long spin. I smashed my previous speed record. When I finished a long and glorious ride, I returned to the basement of our home. I polished the chrome, taking out all the fingerprints, so it shined like a mirror. When I finished buffing out the bike I took one long look at it. I noted the deep burgundy with its decorative gold strips. It was the nicest bike I had ever seen or rode. Then, I gave it to my younger brother. He outgrew his toddler three-wheeler.

Later, my mother told me that was a truly a nice thing to do. I said, "Ya, I lost the bike, but I got something better." She said, "What did you get." I said, "A new best friend." That was my first taste at giving. It is very addicting. Paul in his letter is inviting Philemon to enjoy the same experience. He can gain a brother and the euphoria that goes with it.

My friend took me fly fishing to Pennsylvania because it is the best place in the country—perhaps the world—to catch trout. Fly fish in Pennsylvania, are you putting me on? Should not the best trout fishing be found by taking a bush plane into the remote area of Canada or Alaska? Should we not consider the trout in New Zealand as the best in the world? How do you get great trout in Penn State? The reason my friend is right on this is that the river where the fish live is fed by spring water. It is always cold, clean, and highly oxygenated—perfect conditions to support lots of bug life for fish. When I went to Pennsylvania, I called it the "happy place" because everything is always green from the limitless water supply under the ground—lots of healthy cornfields and happy cows. Even when the rest of the country is in brown with a drought, the "happy place" will always have plenty of great clean water. In the Holy Land where the people of God dwell, they do not have unlimited water under the ground. They depend on rainwater. So they have to store their water in wells and cisterns by collecting the water during the rainy season of winter. So let's say that I am in the Holy Land and I want to do a little cleaning around the house, give my tomato plants a drink of water because they are a little stressed, boil some potatoes for supper, and take a nice bath at the end of the day. I go to my cistern to collect the water I need. I lower down the bucket and…nothing. What? Where is all my water? I climb down the cistern, and I notice a big crack in the wall. What do you think the first thing I am going to do that day? Fix the cistern. I need my "happy place."

The reason I tell you this is because Jeremiah tells the people of Judah that they have a broken cistern. What he means is for them to "fix it, now." Prophetic urgency means putting something off for later is not an option. Of course, Jeremiah is using an analogy to raise the issue of the broken relationship with God. They need to fix it now because, without God, they will be very far from their "happy place." So his point is clear, at least to the ancients, but there is a problem. Relationships are not easy to fix.

My mother had a brother. I never meet my uncle. I have no idea what he looks like, where he lives, and we never received a Christmas card from him, ever. After he argued with his father, my uncle severed his relationship with his family. You would think after fifty years of silence he would say, "Well, I am a lot older now; I am better at life than when I was a teen, and he is my Dad. I should give him a call and take him to lunch. I talked to my mother about this: "I want to meet my uncle, maybe he will want to give me a Christmas present." She said to me, "Oh no, Peter, you do not understand. I will never hear from my brother again." Sometimes the hurt is so deep that the relationship cannot be fixed.

My two friends got married. They were best friends, and they had a lot of fun together. Everyone said that God personally arranged this marriage. They had a couple of arguments, and I don't think they will ever get back together again. It is sad, but sometimes the hurt is so deep that it cannot be repaired.

So let's turn back to Jeremiah who is insisting that we repair the broken relationship with God immediately. So we tell him that it is not so easy. It may take years to repair. So Jeremiah says this to us. "You are right. God is very hurt when we break our relationship with him, but he also can get over it. God is not like us. He does not brood over injuries, He does not harbor a grudge, He is slow to anger and rich in kindness, and He is very humble. Fixing a relationship with God is easy. The most wonderful thing about God is He makes broken relationships easy to fix. It stands to reason that maybe if I had some of His humility and no holding grudges, and some of his slow to anger and rich in kindness and easy going nature, then maybe I can fix some of the broken relationships with my neighbors. And that is the point. If you have a broken cistern, a broken relationship with the divine, fix it now. By being humble and being slow to anger and rich in kindness, you have the tools to do it.

The book of Genesis reports that God walked in the Garden of Eden. I imagine one particular day that God enters the garden and asks, "Where are they? They usually come right over when I come to the garden. The other day Adam and Eve almost ran me over they were so excited. They said, 'we think there is something wrong with the horses, they have very long necks.' They're not horses I explained, they are giraffes. I gave them a long neck so they could eat off the higher branches. And then yesterday they came running to me and said, 'we were swimming in the sea, minding our own business and this monster leaps out of the water.' I said, Oh, I forgot to tell you about that one. That is the whale; it will not hurt you unless I tell it to swallow you. But where are they today?" Meanwhile, Adam is hiding behind a bush because he just ate the forbidden fruit. He is hiding and thinking, "I hope He leaves; I hope God goes away." That is the definition of evil. Evil wants God to depart, disappear, to vanish from us. Grace is the opposite of evil. It wants God to come and stay. That is why Mary was called "full-of-Grace" by the angel. She wanted God to come and stay among us. It was through Mary that we have Emmanuel "God is with us." Maybe that is why history remembers her as the new Eve.

Why am I telling you this, because Paul is writing to the Corinthians and he says to them grace and peace be with you? Let me explain what grace means.

Before the cell phone, before text messaging, before instantaneous information, the The youth group in my parish wanted to organize a dance. "Can we have a dance tonight." I said, "Of course not; we don't have enough time. I have to go to the printer and make posters, then we have to get permission to post them in the schools, and someone has to go around and put them up. You should have asked me a week ago." The kid on the phone replied, "You just have the dance, and we will all be there." I said, "Alright." Around eight at night I walked into the hall, and there were over two hundred and fifty kids. As I was walking around the kids thanked me for giving them their dance. I said, "I didn't do anything. I just said fine, and that was it." When we have grace, that is what we will be saying: "It wasn't me. All I said was yes."

Remember Adam who was hiding behind the bush hoping that God "goes away." Promise you will never find yourselves in a corner and wish this. Never ask God to leave our life, no matter what happens. We need God. We need to be "with him." Always stay with grace, never evil. The next time you read one of the letters of Paul and he writes, "May the grace of God be with you," you will know what it means. You will always want to "be with Him."

Make Sure You Have Good Connections

When God went to Abraham, he said to him, "Go where I tell you to go." God gave Abraham no road map, no money for the tolls, no explanations, and no instructions. Abraham said to God, "No problem." And that is why Abraham is the father of faith. A few hundred years later, God went to Moses and told him to go to Egypt and free the Israelites from slavery. So Moses got up and left for Egypt. No questions, no problems. Well, not exactly. Moses spends the next few chapters telling God why his plan was a bad idea. Moses actually had legitimate concerns. First, he had killed an Egyptian defending one of the slaves, so as soon as he crosses the Egyptian border, they will arrest him. Next, he is never going to have an audience with the most powerful man in the world. He is a former slave. Then, the message is unfavorable. Moses is supposed to tell Pharaoh that he plans to take the slaves, his free labor, and leave the country. Without question, the proposed plan will not go over well with the leader of the world. But let's just say Pharaoh thinks it is a good idea because the slaves could use a change of scenery, Moses will have to lead the Israelites through one of the most feared deserts in the world. There will be no water or food. So Moses tells God: "You plan stinks; it will not work." Do you know what God said to Moses? (Pay attention because this is important) God said, "I will be with you." "When you cross the border, and they come to arrest you, don't worry, I will be with you. When you stand before the most powerful man in the world, and you get stage fright and forget what to say, don't worry because I will be with you. When you give Pharaoh my message, he is going to be very angry, and he will want to see some muscle from me, don't worry because I will be with you. When you leave Egypt you will have to cross the Red Sea, don't worry because I will be with you. When you get into the desert, you will be right. There will be no water, food, or shelter. Don't worry because I will be with you." Moses led the people from slavery to freedom because he heard God say to him, "I will be with you."

So you wake up in the morning and see the news, and that is never good. Then you go to work, and some people don't like you and some who do not appreciate you. Then you come home and open the bills you got in the mail. After you catch your breath after finding out what you owe, you check your voicemail and hear that everyone you know on the planet has a problem, and they need you to fix it. After six days of this you drag yourself back to church, and what is the first thing you hear? The thing you need to hear: "The Lord be with you." So be confident.

Moses said to God, "Your plan stinks, it is not going to work." Do you want to say that to God? Is that your conversation with God? Now we have an alternative response to all the mission impossible scenarios that we meet in life. The Lord is with us. Our most important work is being with the Lord. It is not just a relationship with the one true God but a family made of daughters and sons. We are enriched to have brothers and sisters. Once we have a family, we now can focus on one another: service.

Chapter Eleven

Service

One of the greatest men of service and co-partners in Christ's mission was John the Baptist. It is a good place for us to begin our examination of service. Let us start with John's most recognized work: baptism. Have you ever wondered how John baptized? I used to picture the Baptist as a half-crazy, unfashionably dressed man who had an odd diet. I envisioned that this eccentric would stand in a river up to his knees shouting to the crowd, "Okay, who's the next sinner? I don't have all day." If you were one of the many who made the pilgrimage to the Jordan to be baptized by John in the first century, you would be thinking to yourself, "Well, I may as well get this over with." So, the first thing you do is you take off your sandals and walk down into the Jordan River to meet John in the river.

Since reading the Gospels carefully, I have a different take on what happened to the many who made the quest to the desert for their baptism. All four Gospels claim that John was not worthy to untie the sandals on "His" feet. That would indicate John's regular practice. He was not worthy to untie "His" sandal straps, but that didn't stop him from untying the sandals straps of everyone else. Addressing someone's feet in any capacity in the ancient world was a slave's job. It was below the dignity of a free person. I can imagine Jesus' initial reaction when he watched John kneel before a "sinner" to remove the sandals before baptism. John did not disdain sinners. Rather, he welcomed, served, and assisted them before they began a new life. Jesus would have approved and imitated such a humble and encouraging gesture.

There was another reason why John would approach the sinner first. The Jordan used to be one of the fastest moving rivers on the planet before they added damns. The river's source lies several hundred feet above sea level and empties into the Dead Sea which sits in a basin 1,412 feet below sea level. Needless to say, the river's course has a steep pitch. During the winter rainy season, the Jordan's swift current can be dangerous. In the book of Judges, God had to stop the flow of water in order to give the Israelites safe passage to the Promised Land (Jos 3:16). You did not want to approach this river without supervision and some respect.

John was a humble man, but he was also powerful. He would lower you in the water until you were below the surface, then pull you out of the fast current. That would take a lot of strength. There are two reasons why anyone should fear water: you cannot cry for help under water, and you are unable to breathe. What is the first thing you are going to do when the strong man pulls you out of the dangerous current? Will you give John a bear hug for saving your life? No, you are going to fill your lungs with air. Remember the Greek word that describes that action: "spirit." That breath, or spirit, represents your new life. When you are pulled out of the water, you have been changed. You will never be the same again. What is it about being pulled out of the water that can have such a life altering effect? Perhaps this story will help.

Several years ago my waders leaked. Waders are the outer layer fishermen wear in the water, so they do not get their pants wet. I called the fly shop where I bought my waders, and the store clerk told me to bring them in. I got there, and I recognized him. I had seen him in another fly shop years before. I said to him, "I just called, and I was told to bring in my waders." I showed him where they were leaking and I asked if they could be repaired. He took them in the backroom. After two minutes he came out and handed me a new pair of waders. He said, "Enjoy." I was overwhelmed; I didn't even have a sales receipt. What manager does that? I told him, "Sixteen years ago my father took me fishing at the Salmon River. You managed a fly shop there at the time. You were very good to us. You gave us a map of the river, and you marked on it the best places to fish. You lent us an entrance pass that permitted us to fish private waters, and you asked me if I had waders. When I told you I didn't, you lent me yours. You were very kind to us then, and you are very generous to me now."

He said to me, "One day I fished the rapids in that same river in March. I lost my footing, and the river pulled me under a sheet of ice. I broke through the ice, but by legs and arms were so numb from the ice water, I couldn't use my limbs to pull myself out of the water. I was in trouble. A fisherman saw me, broke his way through the ice and dragged me to the bank. You know, ever since that day, I am different. I spend more time in the garden; I feel grateful because every day for me is a bonus. That is why I am generous." Then he said, "Enjoy the waders and if they leak again, come back here and see me." That is what happens when you are saved. Life is different. If you and I believe that Christ saved us by our baptism, we have to ask ourselves, do we live like we have been saved?

John was a man of service. He committed his life to giving people a new life. He made a difference for people. Those he baptized can now live like they were saved.

Be Committed to Excellence

Quality is always an important element of service. There is bad service and good service. We always want to make sure that our service is exceptional because our brothers and sister we serve are worth it. There was a man who came to Mass every Sunday at my church in Boston. Often he put a one thousand dollar check in the collection basket. This went on for a few months until he started to write checks for one thousand, two hundred dollars. I said, "This is wonderful." After Mass one Sunday this successful businessman came over to me and said, "I am moving to Cleveland for my new job." You can imagine I was not happy to hear this so I said, "Cleveland is not that far away, you could still commute." He laughed, understanding my comment as an attempt at humor. Anyway, I thanked him for his generosity. He said he enjoys being generous not only with his money but also with his time. I asked him more specifically what he did with his time. He said he gave talks to high school seniors on how to be successful in life. So I asked him, "What do you tell them." I wanted to know myself. He said, "I tell them to be committed to excellence in everything they do. I don't care what it is, mow the lawn for dad, clean their room for mom, or write a paper for their teacher. I tell them, if you are committed to excellence in everything you do, you will never have to worry about your future or your career. Success will always follow you."

John the Baptist did not just assemble a mass production of baptisms. He stooped down and untied sandal straps. He served with respect, humility, and solicitous for the dignity of those who came to him even if they were "only" sinners. To think there is no man born of woman greater than John. John sets a new standard by raising the bar above his own status: "The least in the kingdom is greater than he." So be committed to excellence in everything you do, and you will never have to worry about your future as a partner of God.

Partnership Means We Represent God

Service also means that we represent someone or something. Good service means good representation. I went to the shoe store, and the salesman asked, "May I help you?" I said, "I want a pair of black shoes that are going to last, not like the ones I bought at Pay Less and the heel fell off a month later." After he gave me a lecture about good shoes, he said, "I have a nice pair of black shoes, and they happen to be on sale." I tried them on, and he asked me how they fit. I said, "They seem fine." Bending down, he felt the sides of the shoes and said "They feel a little tight. Let me find something wider." I tried them on, and they did feel more comfortable. As we walked to the cash register, he asked me, "Do you have our twenty-dollar-off coupon?" I said, "No, I just happened to walk by and saw the store." He said, "I have an extra one for you." After seventeen years of use. I needed a new pair of shoes. I would have loved to go to the guy that sold me my last pair, but, I don't remember his name. I do not even remember what he looked like. But I do remember the name of the store where he worked. He represented a company in a way that won my respect and my support. We also represent Christ when we serve. This gives us a reason to offer only the best work.

A fly reel jammed on me. I tried to pull it apart by using a lot of force, and I managed to turn a two-piece into a three-piece—I broke it. I looked at the brochure, and it said "lifetime unlimited guarantee." You do not always see that. I bought my first cell phone, and the salesman talked me into buying their "limited guarantee." After a month the phone did not work, so I brought it back to the store. I showed him my limited guarantee, but apparently, they did not cover water damage, so I had to pay full price for another phone—so much for limited guarantees. But an unlimited guarantee is different.

So I called the number of the company that made the fly reel and a guy answered the phone and muttered, "Repairs." I told him my reel broke, and I gave him the model number. He asked, "Name?" I answered, "Oh, my name is Peter Grover" Address? I gave him my address. He said, "Ok, I will send you out a new reel today." I said, "What a minute, don't you want me to send you a receipt?" "No," he replied. "Do you want me to send you the broken reel?" He said, "No, we trust our customers." Naturally, I was impressed, so I asked him. "You don't happen to sell cell phones or cars, do you?" I don't remember the guy I talked to over the phone. I don't have to. I remember the name of the company he represented.

My last name is Grover. I have three uncles with the same name and they are all builders. Needless to say the name also represents a profession. The first day I came to Boston to begin my new assignment was very memorable. I was needed to undertake a restoration

project of the church and seminary there. I had just come from saying a very sad goodbye to hundreds of parishioners from my former
assignment. I had just arrived at my room and I was about to unpack
my boxes, when I turned the light switch on—it was one of those
toggle switches—and sparks spewed about and the light went out. I
sat on the corner of the bed in the dark. That was the lowest moment
of my life. I had left a dream behind to repair a nightmare. But then,
the light came on in my head. The next day, I had dinner with Mom
and Dad. That was when I hired Dad to be the supervisor on the job.
Dad was actually pretty happy about being a part of the project and
he said "Peter we are going to make the church and seminary a beautiful and fully functional place that many will enjoy. This is what we
do as contractors; we fix old buildings, and make them new again.
We are carpenters, you belong to a family of carpenters, all your uncles are carpenters, your brother is a carpenter. Don't forget who you
are, you are a Grover." With a relation you get a name, with a name
you represent something. Do not ever forget who you are or what
you stand for when you partner with God. Many people will be the
beneficiaries of the outstanding company you represent.

In Scripture, you have read the phrase "In the name of the Lord."
This is what the writer means. People may forget our name or our
face, but they will always remember who we represented. They will
remember the name of the Lord. So never forget who you represent.

I was flying back from California. I boarded the plane and sat on
the much coveted aisle seat. Beside me was a ten-year-old boy who
occupied the middle seat. The boy's mom also had a middle seat
across the aisle. She was trying to have a conversation with her son,
assuring him that everything was all right and that she had his books

in her backpack. When I figured out what was going on, I stood up and said to her, "Miss, would you mind trading seats with me?" She said, "No, not at all." She took my seat beside her son and I got to ride back to Boston in the dreaded middle seat. After the flight, when I got to the terminal, the mom was waiting for me. She said, "Thank you, sir. You are a kind and thoughtful man." She may never remember my face, but she will remember that I lived in a way that put others before myself. That is what the name of Christ means. The charity of Christ continues to live in us. And we can be proud to represent such a name as Christ.

Don't Be Surprised that God Has a Dream That Exceeds Our Expectations

God takes pride in his creation. As divine partners we are called to work, but also share in the satisfaction of producing the finest product. Many times in the Gospel, we hear the call to be laborers in the vineyard and to bear much fruit. There is no better illustration of this than Isaiah's parable of the vineyard (Isaiah 5:1-7). God gave the Israelites a vineyard to harvest choice wine grapes. To appreciate such a gift, we need to consult an expert. Once, I had the chance to tour one of the vineyards at Napa Valley. The guide told us that to make world-class wine; you need the perfect conditions. You need to have the perfect amount of rainfall and the right amount of sunlight with a certain range of temperatures. There are only a few places on the planet that provide such conditions. Napa Valley is one of them. Imagine that God gave Israel a "Napa Valley," a rare vine-yard site to harvest grapes that will produce a vintage of world-class wine.

Let's take this a step further and say the Israelites invited the king of Mesopotamia and his entourage to a great banquet. This king, a powerful and feared man, is the ruler of a superpower from the east. There he is, sitting at the Israelite table. Before the food is presented, they serve drinks. Do you think the Israelites are going to serve each of the guests a bottle of Bud Lite? Not when they have world-class wine. They are going to tap one of the many casks of vintage wine that were produced by their God-given vineyard. They fill a glass for the king. The king raised the glass to the light to inspect the body, swirls the wine in the glass, puts the glass up to his nose to smell the fragrance, and then he tastes it. He says to his hosts, "You've got to be kidding. Where did you get this wine? It is fantastic?" The Israel-ites replied: "God gave us a vineyard that produces world-class wine." The king then says: "God must really like you guys; I better start worshiping your God." Know this: God is in heaven hearing the most powerful man on earth speaking great things about God. That is, of course, the divine dream. That is the biblical dream, the dream of the prophets. One day all the nations will gather at one table in peace together (in one accord) praising the greatness of God.

Isaiah recounts the story that God wanted to check out his won-derful vineyard on earth. God must have pictured in his mind the barrels of vintage wine stacked up to the ceiling in the warehouse ready for the feast. He envisioned workers tending to the vines and the soil. He visualized the Israelites in great joy over the gift that He had given them. So the Lord enters His vineyard, and He saw instead that the vineyard he gave was reduced to a valley of weeds: no storage house filled with barrels of wine, no workers, no grapes, no vines. Isaiah said that God was very angry. Why is God so upset? Because there is not going to be a banquet, there is not going to be a moment when the most powerful man on earth is going to be on his second glass of wine saying, "I love your God." There is not going to be an occasion when all the nations of the world are gathered in peace praising God. There is no dream. The reason why the divine dream has been shattered is that no one went out and worked the vineyard.

In the Gospel, Jesus tells the parable of the father who asks his sons to go to the vineyard and work. One son says "yes," but he never went. He represents the Israelites that did not work in the vineyard, which is the reason there is just a valley of weeds. That is not very good. The father has another son, and he asked the second son, and he said "No."

I am sure the son had a good reason for saying "No." "But, Dad, I am getting married tomorrow; I have the two little ones at home; I have to paint the house; I have an important job interview today; I have to finish my research paper." Yes, the son had something important to do, and he told his father "No." But as he was walking away from his dad, he started to think. He began to envision the big picture, the great divine dream that one day all the nations will be at peace sitting at the banquet table eating rich food and choice wines and saying how wonderful God is. As he thinks about the bigger picture of life, he decides that his father had offered him an opportunity to do something great and to be a part of something really big. The son went to the vineyard to work, and now the dream lives on.

We all have important tasks that need to be done. We are all very busy with our lives. Never forget the big picture, the divine dream. Do not forget why we were put here. We can be a part of something very special, and one day we will be seated at the table of the Lord. We must that son or daughter that shares the divine dream and goes to the vineyard and work hard.

If You Want to Prove Someone that You Are a Servant, Just Show Them Your Hands

Good workers have the hands to prove it. My father was not a hugger; he didn't blow loving kisses at us, and he didn't whisper "I love you" in our ears. To show his affection, he shook hands. When I mowed the lawn well, I got a handshake. When I received all A's and B's on my report card, I got a handshake. When I graduated from Princeton with a master's degree, I got a handshake. When I caught the biggest trout in my life, I got a handshake. If I become the Pope of the Catholic Church, I will get a handshake. My entire life of successes can be summed up with a handshake. Why does a handshake from my father mean so much to me? When I was young, I asked him, "Dad, why is your hand so hard?" He explained, "That is because I construct houses all winter. You can't wear gloves when you hammer so I have to hold frozen nails all day. And often my hands get so numb from the cold that the wood would slip and I get splinters. When I carry wood all day and every day in the coldest and hottest days of the year, I get calluses, and that is why my hands are so hard." And I said, "Ohhhhh." I will tell you this. If I ever doubted that my father didn't care or if I ever thought for a second that he wasn't completely dedicated to the family, I would just go up to him and shake his hand. All the doubts would go away.

When we die, we will go up the pearly gates, knock on the door and someone will answer and ask, "What do you want?" We will say we want to enter heaven. Then the person at the door will say, "Do we know you?" When you are asked that question, don't tell him how much is in your bank account, how many books you wrote, or what school you attended. In fact, you don't even have to say a word. Just show him your hands.

There was a young priest who was sent to Brazil. He left his home in Italy, his family and pasta every day. When he arrived, he got into a canoe and paddled up the Amazon River to the first village he entered. He got out of the canoe, baptized some babies, said Mass, and anointed the sick. When he was done, he got back into the canoe, paddled to the next village. He did this for forty years. When his body was too weak to work anymore, he was sent back to Italy. When he got back, God said, "Here is a guy who left his family, friends, and country to serve me for over forty years. Now he needs my assistance. I will send him someone to help him." I was that person. He had the room next to mine, and if he needed anything, he rang a bell. I would drop what I was doing and go in his room. Sometimes he needed a newspaper, help to put on a sweater, or a cup of tea. He would often like to go for a walk, and I would accompany him to make sure he didn't fall. That year I worked very hard on my studies in my room to understand theology. It was in the room next door that I learned how to apply those studies to life. Those who work in the vineyard not only share the divine dream, they inspire others.

Work with Everyone Even if They Are Challenged

Dad employed three supervisors. One guy was perpetually whining. He always had a complaint. The hand saw didn't cut right, the grain was wrong in the wood, the coffee was always cold. Dad had another guy that worked for him who was very bossy. He told everyone what to do, or how they should do it. Everyone's opinion was wrong. Then there was a guy who was in a constant state of happiness. I think he was just ecstatic that he didn't have to sit in front of a screen all day. He was grateful, and always had something good to say. I never got to work with the happy guy. I always teamed up with the bully or the whiner. Why? Because I was able to work with them. I knew how to be patient, and I knew how to keep the peace when they tried to go to war. I knew how to adjust to them, and we always got the job done. My point: God doesn't send us out in a perfect world. He sends us because we are the ones who have the patience, we are the ones who know how to forgive, and we are the ones who are most helpful in difficult times. We are the ones who make the difference in an imperfect world.

This is particularly true in one instance in my life. There was a guy in my father's company who was one of the most cantankerous, angry, bitter persons I ever met. My cousin got so mad at him one day that he took a shovel and filled his toolbox with dirt. Needless to say, my cousin never had to work with him again. I got stuck with him instead. One day we were working on the third floor of an office building, hanging a door. He asked me to go to his truck to get him a drill. I went down three flights of stairs and walked across the parking lot to the truck. I notice that there were three drills, a hammer drill, an electric drill, and one of those old-fashioned hand cranks. Naturally, I grabbed the wrong one. When I returned, he went off on me. He used so many words that were not in the dictionary that the air turned blue. In fact, people were coming out of their offices to see who the troublemaker was, thinking: "What did this kid do to make the poor old man so upset?" I was embarrassed and livid at the same time. I went back to the truck to get the right drill, and I was amazed at what I saw. Right beside the toolbox was a shovel. In fact, it started to talk to me: "Peter, hi there, over here; I am the ticket to the good life. You will never have to work with him again." I considered that option, but there was a better way. When I handed him the right drill, I said in a rather hushed and humble tone, "Sorry about that; I need to pay attention when you speak." He looked up at me and said, "You know, kid, you're alright." Do you know that he never raised his voice with me again? Working with perfect people is easy. I prefer to go where I can make a positive impact.

In Poland, there was a priest who was always getting sick. He had a weak voice and was not a good preacher. The office of personnel didn't know what to do with him, so they sent him to the steelworkers union to say Mass and provide support. He got the assignment that nobody wanted. You can picture this tired, frail, soft-spoken priest addressing all those strong, don't-take-no-nonsense ironworkers. He got up in front of them, and he told them not to let the communists or anyone, for that matter, rob them of their goodness. "Remember," he said, "that we are Polish Catholics and no one can take that from us." The homily inspired the discouraged workers who were forced to labor under the iron fist of communism. They formed a bond among themselves, and they called it "Solidarity."

Soon the enthusiasm spread like fire throughout the nation. Not long after, the whole world was watching. Next, the Iron Curtain came down, and communism evaporated into thin air. It was an amazing string of consequences and reverberations. But if you trace those events back, if you follow the path to the first domino that fell, if you go back to the first action that set everything in motion you will find yourself in the back room of the chancery personnel department with someone wondering, "What are we going to do with this loser?" With God, losers can change the world. This is partnership with God. Flawed people working with God make big impacts.

Keep Doing What You Were Called to Do Because You May Never Know the Impact that You Are Making for Others

Remember the passage in Luke's Gospel that reads, "You are no more than useless servants." It is the one line I love to hate. I never understood why the master would make his poor servant prepare dinner for him after slaving in the field all day. It didn't make sense to me why Jesus would condone such an attitude until I became vocation director of my congregation.

I got a call from someone who wanted to visit our seminary. I scheduled his visit, drew up a schedule, and I cleaned the guest room. After I picked him up at the airport, I got him something to eat. I gave him a tour of the city, I talked to him about his vocation, and I took him to see St. John's Seminary. When his visit came to an end, I brought him to the airport. He shook my hand and said, "I like you guys. I think I want to apply." I was really happy about that because this guy would make a great priest. I said, "Let's keep in touch" and we had many communications over the phone calls and through email. He decided to apply, so things started to get serious. I asked him if he could come up for a weekend to finish up the paperwork and interviews. He said he was about to start finals and he didn't have a lot of money to travel so I said, "No problem, I can come to you." I took the earliest flight to Dallas with a two-hour layover in Atlanta. I got there about noon. We spent four hours in the back of an empty Taco Bell at the airport completing the application. The more I talked to him, the more I liked him. He came from a great family, he was a successful student, and his generosity and care for others were off the charts. When we were done I got up to shake his hand, and he said to me, "Oh, maybe I should have told you this before, but I am looking at another religious order. I like your congregation, but I still have to check out all the options. I will get back to you in a week." I got on the plane for Atlanta. I spent several hours waiting for a delayed flight to Boston. When I finally got to bed, it was one in the morning.

Two weeks later one of the guys in the community, Brother Lou, asked me if the guy from Dallas was still going to join us. I said to him, "No, he is going to join another order." He said, "Oh," and walked away. That is all I have to show for all the phone calls, hospitality details, airport delays, interviews, and frequent correspondence. I got a giant goose egg, no pats on the back, no bump in my pay, no job promotion, no gold star on my head, and no vocation director of the year award. I went to bed that night, and this is what I said to God in prayer. "God, today I worked very hard; it is your church; I am going to bed." That is what servants do. They work very hard, and they can get a good night sleep because they are not the CEOs. Bosses have to worry about the stock market, trade deals, theft, tax laws, making payroll, expanding, hiring, and so forth. The very nice thing about working for Christ is I am a servant, I work hard, but I get a good night sleep.

I am not done with the story. One day after Mass I was greeting the people. "Have a nice day…welcome to St. Clement…I like your sunglasses…." A guy came up to me and shakes my hand. I said, "Have a nice day." He said to me, "Do you remember me?" I said, "Yes, you are the guy from Dallas, we discussed your vocation at a Taco Bell at the airport five or six years ago." He said, "I want to introduce you to my wife and three children." Before he left, he said, "I needed to come back and thank you for all you did for me." Then he turned away, and I never saw him again. I have no clue what I said to him that helped him enough to come back and thank me. I was hoping to figure out what I said so I do not use that line again to other potential prospects. All I know is that God wanted me to meet him. God wanted me to fly down to Dallas to talk to him. Here is what I learned. It is true that we are useless servants. But here is the difference. We are working for Christ. You may never know the good that you are doing. You may never know the difference that you are making for others. All we need to do is this. Work hard and then when we are done, get a good night sleep.

An Ice Cream Man Saved My Mother

My father and I were with my mother's doctor, and we told her that Mom was not eating. She lost her appetite, and the nursing home wanted to implant a feeding tube in her stomach surgically. The doctor turned to Dad and said: "Do not let them put a feeding tube in her. Your wife will no longer need to use the muscles in her throat. Those muscles will grow weak, and she could drown in her saliva." She told us, "You must find something that she likes to eat, something soft that she can swallow." The next day I stopped in JP Licks, a local ice cream chain, and ordered a mocha milkshake. When I got to the nursing home, I gave her the shake. I put a few things away in her room and went to the nursing station to sign in. When I returned, Mom handed me back the cup. It was empty. I immediately called Dad to tell him: "She likes mocha milkshakes." About a dozen milkshakes later, she got her appetite back, and the staff never again mentioned the need for a feeding tube.

About a month later I went back to JP Licks. It was the middle of winter, and I was the only one in the shop. The clerk was a heavy-set guy wearing a Patriots championship sweatshirt. I asked him how he was doing. He shrugged his shoulders and said, "Alright, I guess; what can I get you?" I said, "a mocha milkshake." As he started to fill the order, I said to him, "A month ago the doctors told me that my mother was going to die unless we could find something that she would eat. She completely lost her appetite. The next day, I came in here, and you made me a mocha milkshake, and since then my mother got her appetite and strength back. I wanted you to know that you had a hand in my mother's recovery." As he handed me the milkshake, he said to me, "You have a great day." My point: even an ice cream clerk in the middle of winter can make a difference. We may never know the good we do, or the lives we change by simply serving. This is the advantage of having a divine partner. God arranges contacts, puts us where we need to be at the right time, and provides all the necessary connections that contribute to a powerful story that we could never plan or execute on our own.

My first assignment was in a parish in a small town called Avenel, New Jersey. The first thing we did was send out a questionnaire asking "What do you want us to do for you?" Almost unanimously the parishioners let us know that they wanted a youth program for the high school kids. The request made a lot of sense. There is nothing for kids in Avenel: no malls, no playgrounds, no fields, no fishing. The only thing the kids had to do was hang out on the street, and we all know what disaster that can entail. I said, "Fine, I guess." So we had lock-ins, trips to Six Flags, dances, car washes… it was awful. My hairline immediately started to recede. We also made an impact in the community with projects that assisted the elderly, feeding the homeless, retreats, and educational services. The group required a lot of work, and I wondered at times if it was beneficial. A few years ago I got a Christmas card from one of the first members of the youth group. He sent me a picture of him with his arm around his wife and three children posing in front of their very nice looking home. This is what he wrote on the card: "If you didn't come when you did, this picture would never have happened."

We Do Not Have to Be Experts to Achieve Great Things

Recall the man possessed with Legion. After Jesus and His disciples got out of the boat, a man who was possessed by a legion of demons came out of the cemetery. Michael Jackson's video,

"Thriller," comes to mind. The demons said to Jesus, "Please, we do not want to leave this place, let us go into the swine. What they were trying to avoid was a one-way ticket back to jail. So Jesus said, "Fine, enter the swine." So they entered the swine, and the herd jumped off the cliff and fell into the abyss. The "abyss" is a biblical place that serves as the devil penitentiary. I guess the devils did not outsmart the Lord. They thought they were going to roam freely around the world—not really.

After the swine drowned, the now-unemployed swineherds return to the city to report the bad news to the owners. They were not so happy either now that they are unemployed. Rumors of the event spread and the people of the town needed to see what happened. When they saw the possessed man for the first time without Legion, they were struck with fear, and they asked Jesus to leave their land. Jesus honored their request by getting back into the boat.

I always wondered why Jesus listened to the folks on this particular occasion. Jesus never listened to the synagogue leader who told Him not to cure people on the Sabbath. Jesus never listened to the scribes who counseled Him that He couldn't eat with tax collectors or sinners. He didn't listen to Sadducees who told Him He couldn't forgive sins. He did not take their advice for a good reason. The kingdom of heaven is at hand. There was a lot at stake. Why is Jesus taking advice now? Why leave after one person is freed. The answer is obvious. He finished what He came to do.

What you should then be asking is this: "You mean Jesus crossed the sea in a violent and life-threatening storm to arrive at the other side to assist just one person?" One would think that Jesus had plans to stay at least for a few days and cure a few of the sick and have an opportunity to preach. He leaves after helping a single person. Does that make sense?

As Jesus gets in the boat, the man who was possessed asks if he may join the disciples in the boat. He wants to follow Jesus. I can understand his request. "Lord, I do not belong here anymore. I have no part in a pagan culture, and I do not feel at home in a place like this." It is a sound request, but the Lord tells him no. Instead, he instructs him to go back to his family and show them what God has done.

The Lord returns, and there is the multiplication of the loaves and fish and the feeding of the five thousand families. After everyone is fed, the Lord tells the disciples to get in the boat and go back to the other side again. This time there is a change of plans. They have to go alone, without Him. Jesus needs to ascend the mountain to pray. So the disciples endure another storm without the benefit of Jesus' presence. As they are getting closer to the other side, the storm gets worse. During this gale, the Lord walks on water and, Scripture says that the Lord intended to pass by them. I love that detail. It is as if the Lord is saying, "You guys are too slow rowing, I'll meet you there." Meanwhile, the Apostles think they are seeing a ghost walking on water, and maybe the demons are back. The Lord says again to them "Do not fear; it is I." Once again, He calms the storm.

When they arrive on dry land, and the Lord steps out of the boat, it says in Mark's Gospel that immediately people of the Decapolis recognize Him. Remember, this is the same place where they asked Jesus to leave. Now they want Him? Why the change of heart? They bring their sick and needy to encounter the Christ. How did all these people recognize Jesus as a savior? We are talking ten cities of pagans with their warm reception. Answer: one person. The man Jesus sent back to his family. How was this man so successful? How did he change the perception of the people in a way that they recognized Jesus? Allow me to digress.

I have a good friend who is a Shakespearean scholar. After he had published a book on the Bard, he was interviewed by a newspaper in Cambridge. At the end of the interview, the journalist asked him, "Why do you like Shakespeare so much?" He answered: "If I could write just one poetic sentence like Shakespeare, I would consider my entire life an absolute success."

I have wanted to be a priest since I was in second grade. If you asked me why I wanted to be ordained, I would answer: "If I could just bring one person to Christ, I would consider my entire life a success." The man who was released from his bondage of Legion went out and converted ten cities. How did that happen? Is he a theologian? No. Is he ordained, a bishop, or a cardinal? No. How was he so effective and convincing? All he did was tell the people what God did for him. The strongest argument is always personal testimony. Why does Jesus leave after saving one person from the demons? To show that one person can make a huge impact. And we do not need an ordination, a theology degree, or religious status. Just tell the world what God did for you. That is what partnership will do. God can do a lot with one person. You are that one person. A bad past has no bearing on what you can do now in the present when you partner with God as the man who was formerly possessed by Legion. Do not let the past limit you.

Do you ever play poker? What is the first thing you think when you look at the cards that were dealt to you? "Why do I always get lousy cards?" I was at a convention, and one night we got together with the participants of this particular gathering for a poker tournament. We divided up into groups of five. Someone dealt, and I got a 2, 4, 7, 9 and a jack. That was the worst hand anyone can ever get playing three hand draw. Do you know I made it to championship round? I learned this. The beautiful thing about poker is that you can get an awful hand and still win. It is not about the cards you are dealt; it is how you play the cards. As the Kenny Rogers's song says, "You gotta know when to hold 'em, / know when to fold 'em, / know when to walk away, / know when to run."

Remember the Samaritan woman. If anyone could say they were dealt a bad set of cards, it would have been her. First, she is a Samaritan woman. You can't get lower on the social ladder. In addition to that, she had five husbands, and the one she is presently with is not her husband. She cannot even go to Jacob's well in the morning with the rest of the women to get water to do her daily chores. She must have been tired of the whispering and the finger-pointing, so she goes to the well at noontime when everyone else is gone. There she meets Christ, and from there she is sent to get her husband. Still, she is responsible for an entire village; all the inhabitants are now believers. We are still talking about her today. One "lowlife" can transform a village.

Do you know anyone with a photographic memory? I do. They can be a lot of fun. One day one of my confrères came up to me and said, "Peter, today is your father's birthday; he will turn eighty today." I said, "How did you know that?" He said, "You told me five years ago." At the time he said this, I was preparing for my comprehensive exams. I had to read and remember a stack of books that would fill a small library. I said, "Can I borrow your brain for the exam?" He responded, "Really you want my mind." I said, "Yes, but you can have it back after the exam." I would have loved to have had a photographic memory for the exam, but I don't need it. I passed. It is not about what you have; it is what you do with what you have.

Before God met Moses, he was a former slave and murderer. You can't get lower than that in the ancient world. You may say that he was dealt a bad hand in life. Nevertheless, he is considered the greatest of prophets. What happened? God appeared to Moses and said, "I want to be your God; what do you say?" And Mosses said to God. "What can you do for my people"? And God said, "I can give you all your freedom papers, then I will protect you from your enemies. I will give you food and water in the desert, and I will give you property. Not just any land, but prime real estate. You will be able to plant any crop there, and there will be highways there to connect people to the capital cities of great empires. Everyone will cross into your land and want to spend money there, so your economy will always be rich. So you are going to have great food and lots of money so what do you say, can I be your God"? So Moses says, "Okay, I guess, but what is the catch?" God then said, "All you have to do is partner with me."

Some of us may feel that we were dealt with a bad hand in life. But it is not what you have; it is what you do with what you have. If you have God's Word, you will be able to do many things.

I knew a man who dedicated his life to the healthcare of others. He never got married. He lamented the fact that he never had a family and kids. I said, "Neither did I, but I do not dwell on what I do not have. I spend my time on what I do have, on what God gave me. And God gave you healing powers."

Christ's Job

One other thing to remember is this: Whatever God gives us to do as his co-worker, it will be important. No one can argue that the Lord's work on earth was not important. The reason our work is important is because we were given the Lord's job.

After the Resurrection, Mary thought Jesus was a gardener. Jesus was probably hanging around attending to some of the plants in the garden at the moment Martha walked through. I do that when I am in my garden. Later, Jesus went to visit some friends and got a bite to eat. A week later he had breakfast on the beach with a charcoal fire after catching a boatload of fish. Jesus is acting like a man on vacation. Did it ever occur to you that He did not work after the Resurrection? No more long discourses to the crowds, healings, multiplication of the loaves, or confrontations with the religious leaders. I find that very strange. Think about what Jesus could do in one day of work. He could appear before Pilate after his death and ask him, "Do you remember me?" Think how powerful that would have been. He could have gone to Athens, and I am sure there would have been a few educated philosophers who would have appreciated to know that Jesus rose from the dead. They would have seriously thought about a change of religion. Jesus would be able to do more in one day than all the Apostles could do in years. Is this too much to ask? Why doesn't Jesus work after the Resurrection?

Here is something else to consider. Jesus had a resurrected body, the perfect working machine. Imagine what you could do with a resurrected body at work. No more back pain to slow you down. Or let's say your flight was canceled because of a snowstorm and you will have to miss your important business meeting. No problem, you have a resurrected body. With a resurrected body you will never be late for a meeting again. Or they locked the supply closet, and you can't get in. No problem. You have a resurrected body. You can pass through locked doors. Jesus had a resurrected body. Why did Jesus no longer work? Be sure of this: it was not because he did not love his job. Jesus loved being the Son of man. Once they tore the roof off a house to get to Jesus so they could lower the paralyzed man down. Not only did Jesus forgive the man's sins, but He told him to pick up his mat and go home. That man went back home, sinless as well as walking. Jesus loved His job.

Another time Jesus was walking near the city of Nain, and there was a funeral procession. A mother was on her way out of the city gates to bury her son. There is no pain greater than a parent losing a child. Jesus went over to the body, touched it, and said to the boy, "Get up." He got up. There was probably not a dry eye among the crowd seeing mom holding her boy one more time. Jesus loved His job. Who would not want to do such great things for others? On the day of the Resurrection, He didn't work because he gave us his wonderful job.

At the end of my last assignment, the parish in New Jersey threw me a going away party. There were lots of well wishes, hugs, and tears. Some of the tears were theirs, and some were mine. About a year later, I had to return to the parish. I said, "Hello everyone. It's me." And they said, "Oh, Fr. Peter, we love your replacement. He's wonderful. He knows all the CCD children by name. He is always cheerful and kind. He is just so, you know, great. And we love to spoil him." I turned to Jim, the one that replaced me, and I asked him, "What do they mean by spoil." He just smiled. I said, "I thought so." Then I told him that I wanted my job back. Christ gave up his job on the day of His Resurrection to give it to us.

I got a call from the hospital. When I arrived at the neonatal intensive care unit, the nurse explained to me that a mother and father wanted to have their newborn baby baptized. She said, "The baby is not going to make it. The parents are expecting you in the waiting room." I opened the door, and there was a couple dressed like bikers. They wore dark brown leather pants and jackets, and they had tattoos. Dad was sporting a "ZZ Top" beard. I asked, "Are you looking for the priest?" They stood up and introduced themselves. It turned out that they were among the nicest people. They asked me if I would baptize their baby. I said, "I would be honored." We went into the NICU where the baby was, and we prayed together.

Sometimes when I preside at weddings, baptisms, and first communions, the faithful are often distracted. They are making adjustments to their cameras and waving to friends. So when I say "The Lord be with you" in the context of the liturgy, they never know how to respond. I hear crickets. However, when I prayed with this couple, they were familiar with all the responses. What made them special is that they prayed from the heart.

As I was leaving the unit the nurse accompanied me to the door and said, "We do not expect the baby to live the night." I said, "If they need any support, please call me." I didn't get a call. A week later I was at the same hospital for a different patient. As I was going through the main lobby, I saw the father. I recognized him instantly from the distance because he sported his leather jacket and his distinguished beard. He spotted me and came over as if he were in a hurry. He told me that he and his wife were looking for me all week. He said, "My wife has something to say to you." She was at the other end of the hospital with her back toward us. We walked toward her. When I got close, she turned around, and she was holding a baby in her arms. I was momentarily bewildered. She said, "Right after you left, just after the baptism our little girl started to improve. I wanted you to know that today we are taking her home." I said a prayer, "Lord, I love your job."

We Do Not Just Say "Wow" as a Prayer, We Do It

Remember the one-word prayer, "Wow." We say that when we are noticing God's work. When we work on God's behalf, we are going to do a little wow-ing ourselves. Get used to it.

I was the vocation director. One of my jobs was to advertise in religious periodicals. I didn't know anything about advertising, but I knew someone who did. He said that he could help and invited me to his office. On my visit, I was brought to a conference room with a large oval table. One of his staff asked me, "What exactly are you looking for?" I said, "I am looking for men who are willing to make a sacrifice for others and who are good team players. I am looking for guys that are generous, quick learners, and committed to excellence. I am looking for men who want to make a difference in the world." Everyone around the table smiled thinking, "Yeah, those kinds of guys are highly sought after as husbands, and they also make pretty great CEO's. Good luck because they are in big demand." One of them, Brian, responded, "You are asking for a lot." I said, "Well let me tell you about the seminarians we have now. One gave up a scholarship to a graduate program at Harvard; another had a job that was paying six figures, one of them was the master of ceremonies for the archbishop of Denver when he joined us. I meant to go on, but Brian heard enough and said, "Wow."

Let me ask you this? Did you ever "Wow" Others? You will if you partner with God.

When I was a vocation director, a young teacher called me from Alaska asking if he could visit our religious order. He spent about five days with us. When I took him to the airport, he told me he liked our congregation and wanted to apply. When he finished all the required paperwork, he gave me a call. The only thing that remained was the interview with me. I asked him if he could return to Boston. He told me that he ran out of vacation time and funds to finance the expensive trip. It looked like I had to go to Alaska. I called my father and said, "Dad, I have to go to Alaska on a business trip." My father, who always dreamed about going to Alaska to fish said to me, "I'm going with you." We arrived Saturday night. The next day I had my interview. We then went to his parish. After the liturgy, he said, "I'm going to take you to a nice place to fish." He said it should be pretty good because the salmon are starting to run up the rivers to spawn. When we pulled into his spot, we could not believe what we saw. There were so many fish you could walk across the river on their backs. Every cast we made we had a salmon. The hours passed like minutes, and toward the end of the day, my applicant had to drag us away to see another place. We got in the car and drove for about ten minutes, and he stopped the car. We got out, and we were standing in front of a glacier that ran into a lake. Eagles were flying over the water, and snowcapped mountains were visible in the distance. It was one of the most breathtaking scenes I have ever seen. It was paradise. My father was so absorbed in the moment–his boyhood dream now a reality—turned and said to Sean, the young man applying to the seminary, and said "You want to leave all of this to go to Boston? Are you crazy?" I quickly motioned to my tight-lipped mouth. I had to remind Dad, "Business trip, I'm trying to recruit him to join the seminary in BOSTON." Sean laughed and turned to my father and said, "If God wants me to serve, I am going to Boston." I thought to myself, "Wow." Today Sean is an Oblate priest, and he is the Dean of Our Lady of Grace Seminary. If you partner with God, you are going to "wow" the folks.

It is Not About How You Serve; It Is About Who You Serve

Part of the reason why our work succeeds is because we are serving very important people. Once Jesus said, "Give a cup of cold water to a little one, and your reward will be great." If you consider the value of water and the value of a divine reward, you have to wonder what the connection is. How could Jesus possible confuse the two as being equal? I never really understood that saying until one day. I was sitting at the desk in my office when the mail came. I got a thank-you card from a dad who was grateful for her daughter's wedding at which I had presided a few weeks before. I opened up the card, and a check fell into my lap. When I looked at the amount of the check, I started to laugh. I have never seen so many zeroes. It was a lot of money. I thought to myself. I know I did a good job. I was good, but I wasn't that good. I called the father and thanked him for his generosity that exceeded every expectation. This is what he told me. "My daughter was worth it." I began to realize that my "great job" had nothing to do with the zeros on the check. My service didn't even play a partThe value was placed on the one I was serving.

Jesus once told a parable about those who seek places of honor at banquets. Jesus recommended that we do not go to the head table of honor to find a seat. Otherwise, we may be humiliated when we find out we are in someone else's seat. Rather it is better to go to where those of less social status sit. Why?

Let's suppose I was invited to a banquet in the ancient world. I walk in, and someone generously invites me to sit at a table. I walk to the front of the hall and, I sit down in an empty seat, and the man I am sitting beside is the Roman Emperor, Constantine. He asks me how things are going with the construction of the new church. I tell him "pretty good." "Why is it just pretty good?" he asks. I tell him, "Well, I am running out of money." He asks how much it will cost. I tell him. He mumbles something about pocket change and reaches inside his coat and pulls out his money satchel. Just as he is reaching for the sack, I feel a tap on my shoulder. I turn, and two gentlemen are standing behind me. One says to me, "Father, I am very sorry, but you are sitting in the seat of the keynote speaker." At that moment, the Roman Emperor wants to shake hands with the most important man in the room, the keynote speaker, but he can't because there is a satchel in his hand. He slips it back in his pocket to free up his hand, and I slink away to find another seat. I find one at the last table in the back of the hall.

I sit down and introduce myself to the man next to me. He tells me that the seat that I am sitting in would have been for his wife, but she is in the hospital. He said, "My wife would love you to visit her and offer her a prayer." I said, "I would be honored." I reach into my coat pocket to get a pen and paper to write it down, and I realize at that moment that I am in the right seat. I am the one doing the giving.

I read the parable, and I know exactly why the high priests and the religious leaders want to sit with the high rollers at the front of the banquet hall. When a priest sits at the place of honor, they get Red Sox tickets or a new church boiler donated. In the ancient world, you didn't go to banquets for just the food; you went to make friends with the "haves" because you could get stuff. But Jesus invites us to the last table in the rear because that is where the "have-nots" are sitting. Something happens when we go to sit at the last table. When we sit with the have-nots, we are no longer takers. We become givers.

About a year after I got my driving license, a nice lady from church asked if I would help her at Medfield State Hospital every Sunday morning. She needed a hand getting some of the patients to the main pavilion for Mass. When I got there, they immediately teamed me up with Billy. Billy was a young man who was paralyzed from the neck down. He had limited use of his hands, and he could not talk. The next Sunday I knew the routine. I went to find Billy. He was in his wheelchair fast asleep. In fact, every Sunday when I got there, I found him asleep. During my fourth visit, I was about to leave when the kitchen help dropped off a tray of hot lunch in front of Billy. The aid then left to get another tray for someone else. Naturally, Billy was looking down at the food, but he couldn't feed himself because of his paralysis. So I went over to one of the aides (who was helping someone else) and asked if someone was going to help Billy eat because his food is getting cold. She said that they were low on staff and he would have to wait. I asked if I could I help out. "Sure," she said. So I picked up a fork, harpooned a few stringed beans and lifted it in front of Billy's mouth. He shook his head "No." I tapped the chicken with the fork, and again I got a "No." I said to him, "You're not going for the delicious chocolate pudding before eating your veggies, are you?" That was the first time I ever saw him smile.

It was during that meal that I learned Billy's personality. I discovered that mealtime was his favorite time of day because he loves to eat. I understood that he likes hamburgers, hotdogs, French fries, onion rings, and any dessert with chocolate. It was the first time I heard him laugh and it was the first time he heard me laugh. Just before I left to go home, I told him, "I'm bringing the food next week."

The next Sunday when I went to get Billy, I saw him do something that I never saw him do before. I didn't find him asleep in his wheelchair. He was waiting at the door for me.

In life, we can choose to hang with the haves or the have-nots. If we sit with the haves, we can get stuff. If we sit with the have-nots, we will get fulfilled in life. The workers in the vineyard are there to bear fruit. With God, we have an opportunity to reap a bountiful harvest.

Net Menders

People are drawn to goodness. Some come and join us, and those who are already with us want to stay. If we put this in terms of fishing, some catch the fish and others make sure we do not lose the fish we catch. The Gospel illustrates this very well in Mark, Matthew, and Luke. Jesus is walking along the Sea of Galilee, and he sees fishermen. He calls them. Next, he discovers two others mending their nets. Why does Matthew not just write that they are fishermen? Why does he point them out as net-menders? Because Jesus needs two sets of skills: one to catch the fish and another not to lose the fish after they are caught. Let me explain.

I ran into my fly-fishing friend. Naturally, the first question I asked him was if he has been catching fish. He answered my question by showing me his hands. He had several lacerations on his palms. That was his way of telling me he had been very productive. Fish have very sharp fins.

Picture this: a fisherman pulls up the net full of fish. What are the fish doing at the bottom of the net? They appear to be wiggling. What they are actually doing is they are taking their sharp fins and sawing a whole at the bottom of the net. What good is it to find the fish, catch the fish, then haul the net full of fish out of the water only to lose them all when they slip out of the little hole in the bottom of the net? Net menders take the weakest part of the net and make it the strongest.

If you are catching fish with a net, then you are going to need net-menders. I lived in Boston working as a priest during the clergy sex abuse crisis, the very center of the storm. I asked a pastor how he was doing through it all. He told me, "I worked so hard to give the people a church they can be proud of. I remodeled the buildings, got together a great music program, and we have an exceptional educational program. I spend extra time with families when they need it. Now I lost half the congregation." He made a good point. What good is it to draw in people through our integrity, generosity, and goodwill only to lose half of them? This is the insight that Jesus has in the Gospel where he is looking for two sets of skills. So Jesus calls the net-menders because net-menders repair the brokenness.

As I mentioned above how the city of Corinth is one of those rare cities that has both a sea on the east side of the city and a sea on the west, something like Cape Cod, Massachusetts. The plan was to dig a canal so that boats can take a shortcut from one sea to the other. It would save sailors the trouble of negotiating very dangerous waters around the Greek peninsula, a navigational nightmare. They never made the canal in the first century, but that did not stop sailors from going to Corinth and dragging their boat across the land to the other side. So Corinth was at the crossroads of the Roman Empire. It is here that Paul founded a church. He wrote to the Corinthians and said to them, "I hear that there are divisions among you," Of course there are divisions. They are at the heart of the empire. There will be disagreements and differences. Paul then said to them, "Be united." But that is not the word he used. He used the same word that was in the Gospel: "mend your nets." A mended net means the most vulnerable and weakest part of the net has now been re-tied in a way that makes it the strongest point. Often the weakest joints can become the most united places as long as there is a net-mender that knows what he or she is doing. We often experience broken relationships like those that the Corinthians experienced. Paul tells us brokenness can be mended.

Fixing brokenness is not so hard. Jesus wants us to have two skills in place. Drawing people to the Church through our generosity, sacrifice, and forgiveness, and also mending the nets, repairing broken ties.

The Father Passes the Job to the Son

In the introduction of the book, I mentioned the role of the ancient father. His job is to give the kids an inheritance. He does this for selfish reasons. His good name, his work, and his reputation live on in the kids. When the Israelites call God, Father. They have this in mind. God's name, work, and reputation live on. That is why God calls himself the God of Abraham and the God of Isaac. I experienced this father and son relationship on many occasions.

One time, Dad and I were fly fishing, and it started to rain. Dad went back to the truck and took off his waders. I asked him, "Are you quitting now"? He told me he didn't have a rain jacket and it was cold. I now was informed as to what I could give him for Christmas. So I went to a fly-fishing shop to buy him a jacket with the extra pockets and gadgets that are useful to fly fishermen. There was a vinyl jacket without a hood, inexpensive but not very sturdy. Then I looked at one that had a nice hood system to keep out the rain. It also had a cuff that would not allow rain to run down your arm when you raised your hand to cast. It was a great jacket but a little over my budget. I needed to think for a minute. In the meantime, the owner of the shop came over to see if I needed some help. We started talking about fly fishing. We had a good conversation about places to fish and fishing flies that surely worked. He told me about the ups and downs of having a fly-fishing business noting how kids do not fish because they prefer video games. Finally, he asked me what I did for a living. Truthfully, I told him I was a priest, and I had a church in Boston. He said, "Oh."

I finally decided to get the good jacket. I only have one father. I will just have to give up coffee for the rest of my life. When I got to the cash register, there was a girl there, but the owner came over and said, "I will take care of this one." He rang up the jacket, and I saw the price in the register window. I took out my wallet and started to count the money, and he said, "Wait, I'm not done yet." He clicked a few more keys, and the number in the window drastically changed from $300 to $80. I said to him, "What happened?" He said, "I just gave you a discount." I said, "I don't think this jacket is on sale." He said, "Father, I always support you guys. You come back anytime." When I left, I thought to myself, "I know where I am going to go Christmas shopping next year." So the next year I went back. When I got there, I looked around, but the owner wasn't there. I thought, "Oh no, this is not good." I even went over to one of the hired hands and enquired about him. He said, "Oh, that is my father, he is now enjoying retirement." I said, "Well, good for him." I got some gifts and brought them to the counter to check out. There was a woman at the register, but the son came over and said to the cashier, "I will take care of him." He rang me up. It came to about $200, and so I pulled out my wallet to pay. He said to me, "Wait a minute. I'm not done yet." He then clicked a few more numbers and said, "That will be $50. I said, "I didn't think any of this stuff was on sale?" He said, "It's not." He pulled off a 9x11 sheet of paper taped on the cash register and said, "Dad left me a note to remind me to give you a nice discount. Come back anytime, and we will take care of you." I miss seeing the father, but I don't miss his kindness or his generosity because he passed on to his son.

I was fishing with my father. We were at Barnstable Harbor, and a dory pulled up to the boat ramp. It had a wide open pit, a milk crate for a seat and a motor. Its sheer simplicity allowed the boat to hold a number of large bins. We went over to check out the bins to see what he caught. They were filled with horseshoe crabs. I heard that they use them for medical purposes. My father, who knows how to catch a lot of fish, asked the man, "How do you catch horseshoe crabs?" The man answered, "If I told you how, I would have to kill you." He explained that he got the knowledge and skill from his father.

Back in the ancient world that is what dads did. They passed on their trade and skills to their kids so that they would have a successful living. Everyone would know whose son he was by what the son could do. I bet if I went into the coffee shop and said, "Hey everybody. I just saw a guy with a boatload of horseshoe crabs." The dad would put down his coffee and say, "That must be my son." He would know who he was by just saying what he did. Who else knows how to catch horseshoe crabs? God made us in His image so that we would do His work. We have the DNA; let's use it.

There is a room in the basement of the church where people only enter twice a year: once to take the Christmas decorations out and the other time to put them back. There is a table in there, so I go to this room because I know no one will find me. Even my cell phone doesn't work in there. I sit at a table, take out a hook and tie some flies for my fishing. I did not buy the hook or the feather. My friend Jack gave them to me. He is the one who taught me how to tie flies. When he was in the final stage of cancer, he gave me a call and asked if I would give the eulogy at his funeral. I told him I would be honored. He also told me that I was going to be in his will. I was at a loss for words. I have never been in someone's will. Sure enough, after my friend died, I was in his will. No, I didn't get a car, no property, and I didn't get a large sum of money... I will spare you the suspense: I got fishing hooks and feathers. Why would my friend give me fly-tying material? He knew I wouldn't sell it to a local fly shop for a few quick bucks. He knew I would appreciate them and use them. I am sure he is looking down from heaven and smiling, knowing that his legacy did not die with him. It lives on in me. Scripture says that Christ left us a memorial. I think of a memorial as a legacy. We miss Christ when he used to walk our streets, but we do not miss his generosity or spirit of sacrifice because it lives in us. And we should never forget that.

Finish the Job

When we work for God, we do not want to quit too soon. Sometimes we get tired and we do not always see the results. We can get discouraged and loss energy. It is important to preserve to the end. Finish the job. Remember, the most important time of the workday is the last hour. That is when you finish the job. At my first assignment, I was a Director of Religious Education: DRE. There was a storage room full of junk. I don't like stored unusable things, so I got rid of everything and the new space made a nice room for the teachers. I showed the space to one of the instructors, and she said, "My husband is a painter; let him paint the room." One Saturday morning he came over. I had the supplies ready: paint, fresh paintbrushes and rollers, a bucket of water, and drop cloths. He was impressed at my diligence. I told him that I wouldn't be able to help him. I had two weddings, Masses at multiple locations, and baptisms that weekend. Monday morning, I went to the room, and I was rather pleased. The walls looked fresh and clean. He did a great paint job. There were no roller lines on the walls. The windows and baseboards were cut in nicely. There was only one problem. He didn't clean up. He didn't put the covers back on the paint cans. The brushes were ruined, the roller and the pan was bathed in dried paint. There were dried-up paint drips and spills on the floor. I had to spend hours cleaning up the mess. After I scrubbed away the last drop of paint from the concrete floor, I thought that it would have been faster and easier if I painted the walls myself. The most important hour of work is the last hour.

Jesus agrees. He told a parable of a man who hired workers for his vineyard at the last hour of the day. Why would anyone hire someone to work for just one hour? The last hour is the most important hour. The guys who were working in the field all day in the hot sun are not going to put away the tools and clean up. The owner is going to wake up and find that the harvest was not stored away properly. He will see the tools are lying around in the field getting rusty, and the wheelbarrow has a flat tire. The wise owner of the vineyard hires a few guys at the end of the day to finish the job, fresh and ready to work. They will secure the food that was collected so the insects and animals can't get at it. They will put away the tools and fix the wheelbarrow if needed. The last hour is the most important hour. In fact, it is so significant that the last hour workers get the same pay as everyone who worked all day.

Who in the Bible represents the last hour worker? Joseph of Arimathea. He showed up at the last hour of the day when Jesus died on the cross. It was not easy work, and he was pretty much alone. He had to secure permission from Pilate, which means dealing with layers of government bureaucracy. Once he got permission, he had to shop for a burial cloth, ointment, and provide a tomb—all of which are costly items. Then he had to take the nails out of the Lord's hands. I do not have to point out the emotional cost of such a task. These are the hands that raised a dead girl back to life, the hands that touched the leper before he was made clean, the hands that broke the two loaves and fed thousands, and the hands that made mud that cured a blind man. His enemies snuffed the life out of the most compassionate hands ever to have blessed the world. After that, Joseph of Arimathea must bury the body before the Sabbath begins. As he is doing all of this, little does he know that he is preparing the Savior of the world for His Resurrection? He has to fill the tomb if there is going to be an empty tomb three days later. He was the worker of the last hour of the most important day ever recorded.

Do you remember the last words Jesus spoke before He died? "It is finished." Why did He say that? I think He wanted us to hear him end his life by saying the word "finished." He wanted us to know that finishing the job is the most important part of the job. And Jesus finished the job. He didn't come down from the cross as the opponents suggested him to do. He stayed and finished. Not long before Jesus died, He told His followers "to be perfect as my heavenly Father is perfect." That is quite a tall order. I don't think I was ever perfect in my entire life. I don't think I ever saw anyone do anything perfectly. The Greek word for "perfect" means to "finished." It was the same word Jesus spoke before His last breath on the cross: "It is finished." In other words, Jesus wants us to finish the job. That is the kind of perfection he wants us to have. We are baptized into Christ: finish the job. We were called to be His disciples: finish the job.

People Notice Hidden Goodness

One vacation, Dad and my brother went to Maine to hit the mountainous woodlands. The first night we stopped for ice cream. The girl at the window asked, "Will this be on one bill?" I handed her a twenty. When she gave me the change I started to separate the money to put some in the tip jar. Before I reached for the jar, she turned around and went to get the ice cream. I was hoping she would see me put the money in her jar so she would know that we "flat-landers" are also nice people. I even thought about waiting until she came back, but I put it in while no one was looking. She finally came with the ice cream. I thanked her and then she said to me. "No, thank you," and she pointed to the tip jar. How did she know? Does she have eyes on the back of her elbows? I suppose she is not working hard just for the pay. She is there for the tips, and apparently, she is keeping a close eye on that jar. Hiding good deeds is difficult.

I live in a fairly large community. When something breaks, like a vacuum cleaner, there are three options.

Option one: put it back in the closet broken.
Option two: attach a sign that reads "Out of Order."
Option three: Fix it.

Last spring, I needed to photocopy the homework for my class. It is my personal opinion that photocopy machines have a built-in stress detector. They know when you are in a hurry, or that you have to get a copy done immediately because the bishop is on hold, or there is a church full of people waiting for the opening hymn to be distributed. So there I was in front of the photocopy machine. I pushed the "on" button to make copies, and I hit the jackpot. Every warning light started to flash: No toner, no paper, paper jams every-where, call for service." At that moment, I was tempted to act on option one, which is to leave the scene immediately and let someone else deal with the problem. I decided instead for option three, which means no one will ever know I fixed the copier. After I made all the necessary warning lights go out, I finally started to get my copies.

Someone came by just at that moment and asked me, "Oh, did you just fix it?" Which prompted me to think of two questions: "How did you know it was broken, and how did you know I fixed it?" It goes to show you that goodness is hard to hide. Think of all those unnoticed and thankless jobs.

If We Notice, then God Notices

Take a look at the widow who put the coins in the treasury. Jesus noticed, but how? If you look at the fingernail of your pinky finger, you will have an idea of the size of the diameter of a Roman penny. If you hold the penny between your two fingers, you will completely cover it. It will not extend outside of your fingers because it is so small. No one saw the widow put in the two copper pennies in the treasury because they were too small to see. Yet, Jesus knew. He knew that she was more generous than all of them because she gave everything. Goodness is often hidden, but God will always see it because God reads the heart, the home of goodness.

Chapter Twelve

Let God Finish the Story

Often times we get discouraged. Things do not always go as we plan. We do not fare well in the midst of chaos. We may not always have a good plan, but it is better than chaos. With God, everything that happens is part of the plan. There is no chaos with God. There have been times when I had to thank God for getting me through the storms of life. This was true in one particular occasion.

You would think the thunderstorm would just keep moving up the road, but it just lingered around all day. It was a true thunderstorm: loud thunder, lightning, and lots of rain. Naturally, there was a flood in the basement. I was wearing my fishing waders, and I was frantically trying to bail out the basement. The water came in faster than I could get it out so at a certain point in time I threw my hands up in the air, and I said, "That's it; I'm leaving. I have a baptism at Saint Cecilia's Parish." When I got there, the dad of the baby said, "We have to wait, for the rest of the family; you know the rain and all." I thought to myself, "I hope I don't have to wait too long or I am going to watch my church float down Boylston Street.

So there I was standing near dad. He was holding his baby in one hand and a bag in the other. He was trying to get the camera out of the bag to replace the batteries by flipping the old ones out and inserting new ones—not so easy when you are holding a baby in one hand. Finally, he swings his baby into my chest and says, "Father, you hold him." There I was holding this very cute baby. The little guy reached up with his hand and squeezed my nose. He was laughing while doing this. "Oh, so you think it is a toy, huh." While the baby was having a good time with my face, someone in the family noticed and said, "Oh, look, the baby likes the priest." They took out their cameras, and they started taking pictures. I got to hold the baby for two minutes. Then the others arrived, and it was time to start, so I handed over the baby to the father. After the baptism, I went into the sacristy and prayed.

I said to the Lord, "You planned that. You knew I was having a rough day, and today I got to hold a baby." That may not sound like much, but it was to me. The two minutes were special because I do not get to hold babies. When I do, the babies see my black suit, black shirt, and white collar, and they know instantly they're in the arms of a stranger. They immediately start crying, wrangling and trying to get out of my arms. Mom or dad always sees the exasperation in their baby, and they draw near to take him or her out of my arms. It leaves me feeling a little embarrassed and rejected. That's why I never get to hold babies. On this day, I got to hold a baby.

In the letter from Peter, he says we must endure some suffering so that when God's glory appears we may rejoice (1 Pet 1:7). It is a great line. What exactly is glory? The Hebrew term *kabod* comes from the word "liver." What does liver have to do with God? The liver is the heaviest organ in the body. God is invisible so if God wants us to see him; he has to put on some weight. When God is most visible is in suffering. That is, God can be most perceived when he lifts us up in time of discouragement, sadness, or suffering. It is in the time of difficulty that God is most visible.

Remember the Christmas story: God sends His Son into a tumultuous world. He doesn't send Him riding in a fiery chariot with a sword in hand to rescue us. He sends Him as a baby. You will find God in small and concealed forms, which are hidden from the wise and the intelligent. So when you are having difficulty, we ought to re-read Peter's first letter. In it he tells you that when you are suffering, look for the glory, look for God who wants to be visible. It is when we suffer that He comes to lift us up.

God Watches Out for Us

My parents had a family cat that made it clear that she did not want to be petted or cuddled. I believe I know why. My mother used to pick up the cat and give her long hugs saying, "Oh, you are soooo cute." I used to look in the cat's eyes during these moments and see pure hatred. So one day I went into the house and the cat is lying on its back on my brother's lap purring, mushy, and loving. Stunned, I said to my brother, "How did you get the cat to do that?" My brother, who suffers from bouts of depression said, "The cat always seems to know when I am having a bad day. She will never leave my side all day." I thought to myself, "If a cat with a personality disorder can feel for a human being and have compassion, imagine how much God is willing to come to someone in need."

When the cat died, naturally we were all really sad—my brother was crushed. This cat had a special gift. So I asked dad what he was going to do, he said, "I am going to get another cat for your brother." A few weeks later, my brother called while I was in the office. I asked my brother about the cat. He said, "Peter, I don't need to have a bad day for the cat to like me. This one likes me all the time." I was so happy to hear what he said, that I had to tell the first person I saw who was Carol, our office manager. Carol knows my brother because he calls the office often. After I told her, she said, "You see, God is watching out for him."

The Key to Successful Waiting: Let God Finish the Story

When they laid Jesus in the tomb, everyone was sad. Why? He just saved the world on the cross. So why is everyone desolate? They are gloomy and depressed because they did not let God finish the story.

A few seasons ago Tom Brady tossed an interception near the end of the fourth quarter at Gillette Stadium in Foxboro, Massachusetts. He put the ball into the hands of the visiting team who were already winning the game. Forty thousand fans left the stadium. Since there was only a minute left in the game, it made sense to depart and get a jump on the traffic. They were all probably very disappointed and didn't want to hang around to witness the inevitable. Forty thousand fans also missed one of the best and most exciting comebacks in the franchise history. Tom Brady and the Patriots somehow got the ball back and marched down the field into the end zone. Forty thousand fans missed out because they didn't let Tom Brady and the boys finish the game.

At another time, the day after the Super Bowl, I called Dad, a Patriot's fan, and I asked him, "What did you do when the Patriots were down 28-3 late in the third quarter?" He said, "I turned off the TV in disgust and went to bed." And Dad missed out on the greatest comeback in Super Bowl history because he didn't let coach Bill Belichick and the Patriots finish the story.

At the end of my first year in the seminary, I went to the Rector's office for my evaluation. It didn't go very well. He said my grades were low, and the staff didn't think I could finish the studies in philosophy and theology. Even though they decided to give me one more semester, I was devastated. I remember going to the church after the meeting, and I put my head down. I said to God. "I thought You wanted me to be a priest. It was You who instilled in me the desire since I was in second grade. Did I get the signals mixed up?" God then spoke to me. He said, "Peter, Peter, I am not done. Will you let Me finish the story?" I said, "Yes, You can finish the story."

Many years later after I was ordained, I was driving out to St. John's Seminary to teach New Testament Greek to the seminarians. My confrère, David Beauregard, a Shakespearean scholar, was also a teacher at St. John's. While we were at a stop light, I turned to him and asked, "Do you remember my first year in the seminary when you and the staff wanted to kick me out because I was not smart enough? Did you ever think back that it would be me who would be going to St. John's to teach? Of all the great students you had over the years, did you ever think that it would be the two of us to represent our community at St. John's as professors? Did that ever come to mind?" He turned to me and said, "That was God." After he said that, God spoke to me again. He said, "So, what did you think of my story." I said, "It was a little rough, but I love the ending."

Conclusion

Partnership is the powerful story about you teaming up with God. Your limitations are not obstacles in this relationship. God becomes more visible, more obvious when the odds are entirely against you. When you commit to God, you are putting your talents, your skills, and your gifts in God's service—and remember, it does not take much to show the world the greatness of God. God can do a lot with "crumbs:" Phillip's five barley loaves, Peter's net, Simeon's bent arms, Elizabeth's sterile womb, and David's slingshot. The story may have ups and downs. Great narratives always do. But please, let God finish the story. In the end, God will shine, the world will be blessed, and you will be doing what you were made to do. You will have no regrets because your life will be entirely fulfilled.

www.ingramcontent.com/pod-product-compliance
Lightning Source LLC
Chambersburg PA
CBHW070028100426
42740CB00013B/2626